Publishing Poetry & Prose In Literary Journals

by

Writer's Relief, Inc.

*Helping writers prepare and target their submissions
since 1994*

TITLE: Publishing Poetry & Prose In Literary Journals
Copyright: Writer's Relief, Inc.
Published: March 2015
ISBN: 978-0-9913015-5-3
Publisher: Writer's Relief, Inc.

Published by: Writer's Relief, Inc., Wood-Ridge, NJ 07075

Table Of Contents

Introduction: Who We Are And Why You Should Listen To Us

Writer's Relief is an author's submission service, and we've been helping creative writers make submissions since 1994. We're a highly specialized service with expert knowledge of the publishing industry.

We help poetry, short story, and essay writers get published in literary journals, and we help book authors find literary agents.

Our work is personalized, careful, and precise—we're not a "submission factory" and do not support any kind of submission spam. We love writers, and it's our goal to see our clients get published. That means we take a personal, hands-on approach to helping our clients make submissions.

We also do a fair amount of congratulating, advising, strategizing, encouraging, consoling, and cheering on. We have seen countless clients published in literary journals over the years, with many nominations (and even a few wins) for major literary prizes. We've helped our clients answer many of the tough questions that can arise when submitting to literary magazines, such as:

- What is considered previously published writing? Is it "published" if I posted it on my blog or Facebook page? Will literary journals consider it for publication?
- How long do I wait before I follow up with an editor?
- Should I submit to lesser known literary magazines that are more likely to publish my work, or should I hold out for the top publications in the industry?
- What can I do to make my submission stand out?
- What should I watch out for when I start submitting? What are the red flags?
- What should I do if a literary journal asks to publish my writing but doesn't give me a written contract?
- Can I submit my revised work to literary journals that already considered the original version? How?

Now, after many years of offering our expertise to the writers on our very limited and exclusive client list, we have decided to pass our expert advice along to you.

How Is This Book Different From Every Other Book About Literary Journals?

This is NOT a market book filled with specific listings of literary journals or magazines. There are plenty of those already. Plus, our private database is overflowing with notes on the editorial preferences of literary journals gleaned from their many personal comments to our clients since 1994. We couldn't fit all our detailed listings in a book even if we wanted to!

This is a book for writers who want to get published in literary journals by developing an effective, long-term submission strategy.

The advice in this book can help any author—whether you are a new writer who doesn't really understand how literary journals work and is afraid of being scammed or whether you are a veteran writer trying to figure out why you're getting so many "nice rejections."

You will notice a little repetition throughout this book; this is deliberate. We believe that some repetition helps with memorization; it makes things stick. But also, when you return to this book later on trying to find that "one thing" you meant to remember, you'll have an easier time of locating what you're looking for.

Trust Your Instincts

If you read enough about the publishing industry, or if you attend enough writing conferences, you will know that there are conflicting opinions about a lot of the topics we cover in this book. Everyone has his or her own idea about what's best.

What we offer readers is a perspective that is uniquely pro-writer (as opposed to pro-agent or pro-editor). While you may not agree with all of our recommendations, we hope we can offer food for thought. Ultimately, you must make your own way within the publishing industry using your instincts as your guide.

We've been working with writers for many years, and it's always a thrill when one of our clients calls us to say, "I got another publication offer!" Our clients have ranged from career academics, to professional bestselling novelists, to promising but unpublished writers. Some clients have amassed many publications in literary magazines and proceeded to release collections with great publishers. One client sent us 100 bottles of beer to celebrate his 100th publication... Don't worry! We didn't drink them on the job—or all at once!

We would not mislead our clients and say that getting published is easy and straightforward. An effective submission strategy is NOT a one-time effort. Making a few rounds of submissions every once in a while also isn't a strategy, it's a crapshoot. To really be effective in making submissions and getting published, you need to have a plan. You must have the mind-set that regular, habitual submissions are as fundamental to your writing goals as your actual writing (because the more doors you knock on, the more will open). If you want to be published in many journals, you must submit to many, many journals—regularly, professionally, and enthusiastically.

In this book, we'll teach you our methods. Our system might not work for everyone, but learning what we do will help you determine what works best for you. Our expert, personalized market research connects our clients with the literary journal editors who are most likely to enjoy their writing. And we know that our clients' submissions go out into the world with the best possible formatting and proofreading. We love writers and are proud of the work we do.

If you're interested in knowing how Writer's Relief can help you (we can manage as much or as little of the submission process as you like), just find us online or give us a call. We're easy to get in touch with. You'll also learn a lot more about us as you read this book, since we will often present our own thoughts and strategies to give you a complete picture of your options.

But of course you do not *need* a Writer's Relief submission strategist managing your submissions to literary journals in order to succeed. If you've got the energy, dedication, focus, talent, and time for making submissions, you'll be fine. If you would rather have some help, you know where to find us.

For now, just enjoy this book. We hope it will answer your questions about finding and submitting to literary journals.

Please contact us and let us know what you think! We would love to hear your story about connecting with a literary journal. We might even use it on our website!

Happy reading!

Ronnie L. Smith

Ronnie L. Smith, President
Writer's Relief, Inc.
(866) 405-3003
www.WritersRelief.com

Part One

Welcome To The World Of Literary Journals

What They Are, What They Do, And What They Mean To You

Literary Journals + Your Writing Career = A Match Made In Heaven?

What is a literary journal (aka literary magazine)?

Not to be confused with commercial magazines that appear on newsstands, a literary magazine is a publication that focuses strictly on creative writing. Literary magazines can be in print or online and can be associated with a university or an independent literary press. There are thousands of literary magazines in existence today, but the majority of them rarely appear for sale in bookstores.

Funding for literary magazines usually comes from monthly or yearly reader subscriptions (which may number a few hundred subscribers to tens of thousands). Many literary magazines are also funded by government and private subsidies that support the arts. More often than not, literary journals are unable to pay their contributors. They exist to showcase writing and artwork that would otherwise not find an audience in mainstream, commercial publishing.

What Is The Difference Between A Literary Magazine And A Literary Journal?

Sometimes a tabloid-sized publication may be referred to as a magazine, and a perfect-bound publication may be referred to as a journal, but the terms are used interchangeably by most people. You may also see the term "lit mag" as shorthand.

What Do Literary Magazines Publish?

Literary magazines typically publish short fiction, poetry, creative nonfiction, book reviews, and sometimes art and photography. Some magazines specialize only in poetry; others will publish only stories. The focus can range from general literature to specific topics, such as nature, politics, or religion.

Overall, literary magazines and journals tend to have a literary feel—emphasis is on style and insight rather than a fast-moving plot intended for escapism. However, there are some literary magazines that cater to readers of a specific genre fiction (horror, mystery, science fiction, etc.).

What Are The Best Literary Magazines?

While there are many renowned and respected literary magazines that have been around for decades, it is best to focus less on which are the "best" and more on which are the best for your work.

Do You Need A Literary Agent To Get Published In A Literary Magazine?

Literary agents act as writers' representatives. Agents work on commission and tend to focus on selling full-length books to publishers. A few might help well-known, established authors publish their work in high-circulation magazines like *The New Yorker*, but this is a perk reserved for authors who are famous enough to merit it.

Because literary journals don't pay much (if anything at all) and literary agents work on commission, most will not find it cost-effective to submit your writing to lit mags for you. Writers who publish stories, poems, or personal essays in literary journals generally do not need the services of literary agents. You can submit on your own.

To learn more about agents, visit our website and check out *The Writer's Relief Field Guide To Literary Agents*.

How Can I Help Ensure That The Lit Mag Market Remains Strong?

We love lit mags.

And if you're a creative writer, we hope you do too. Literary journals are the beating heart of American stories, poems, and essays. Most are purely labors of love.

But lit mags face extraordinary challenges. The readership for literary journals isn't exactly what you'd call "mainstream" or "commercial." They're incredibly important, showcasing the best writing by new and veteran authors—and yet, compared to glossy magazines, their readership is small.

Right now, literary magazines are the BEST place for writers to publish poems, stories, and personal essays/creative nonfiction. And we're incredibly thankful for them. We hope writers, readers, and editors can continue to work together to ensure an even brighter future for these important publications.

Here's how you can do your part. Consider it the Golden Rule of Serious Writers:

If You Want To Be Published In Lit Mags, Read And Support Lit Mags.

HINT: Want to find some great literary journals to read, subscribe to, submit to, and support? Then, read through our Lit Mag Spotlights on our blog. We hope you'll support these amazing editors who have dedicated their time and talent to supporting writers like you.

Why Focus On Literary Journals?

Some writers ask us why they should bother submitting work for publication in literary journals since lit mags rarely pay their contributors.

There a many reasons to seek out literary magazines, even if you're not getting paid.

1. Being published shows literary agents, editors, and potential employers that you can manage submission deadlines and guidelines and that you are a serious writer. You establish yourself as savvy and in-touch by being published in literary journals. If you're thinking about trying to publish a book, having publication credits in a lit mag will lay the groundwork for a career in lengthier fiction.

2. If editors publish your short works, it means they believe their readers will enjoy your writing. The fact that editors are enthusiastic about your writing can help when you're trying to get an agent or applying for a master's degree.

3. Having credentials in the small press market may help you stand out from the competition. Most publishing industry professionals are aware of how difficult it is to secure one single publishing credit. A solid bio tips the scales in your favor.

4. Not only will publishing your shorter works make you a more interesting prospect, seeing your writing published is emotionally rewarding. Acceptance letters from literary magazines go a long way toward keeping you motivated.

5. Publishing in literary magazines might directly help you with getting an agent. A number of our clients have been approached by New York agencies because an agent read a story in a literary magazine. Getting your work, your name, and your bio out there can get you noticed in much the same way a model might get noticed simply by hanging around at the hottest nightclubs (except in a much nerdier, bookish way).

6. By publishing in lit mags, you begin to build your reputation as a writer. Most importantly, you are getting your writing out where people can actually read it. It's not doing anyone any good if your best work is hiding under your bed or on your hard drive.

The Changing Publishing Landscape And You

With the advent of online literary journals, writers seeking reputable and well-known venues to publish their work are *no longer confined to print.*

Yes, you read that right. If you're just entering the world of publishing, prepare for a digital experience. Online literary magazines now coexist with (and in some cases, taken the place of) print magazines. This is *good* news for writers of short stories, essays, and poems.

The Historical Stigma Against Online Publications

In the early days of the Internet (when Writer's Relief was just starting out back in 1994), online publications of short prose and poetry were considered by some writers and readers to be lesser publications than print journals. However, now that the Internet has come of age, publishing your writing in reputable online journals and other venues no longer carries a negative stigma. Many publishing industry experts believe that traditional literary magazines will convert increasingly to online-only models. The trend has already started to take hold.

Why Many Literary Magazines Have Already Gone Online

As we've mentioned, there isn't a lot of money to be made in short stories and poetry because literary magazines often operate on a very limited budget.

The recent economic conditions only made the situation more difficult; many, many literary magazines have closed their doors. At Writer's Relief we are also tracking an alarming number of literary magazines that are "on hiatus" or "indefinitely closed for submissions."

Print magazines that were under financial duress during the economic downturn had a choice: adapt or fail. To cut costs, editors who chose to persevere turned to the final frontier in publishing: the Internet. Without the high costs of printing, binding, and mailing, literary magazines can operate on an even smaller budget.

For that reason, there are more reputable literary magazines online now than ever before. And conversely, there are fewer print journals than there were a few years ago.

Writers who have been trained over the years to respect only print publications may find it difficult to believe that online publications and print publications are now on equal footing. Some writers may prefer to hold a physical publication in their hands. But, just as literary magazines have had to adapt, writers need to adapt as well. The practical benefits of publishing online may outweigh any lingering emotional reservations.

Top 5 Ways Publishing With Reputable Online Venues Can Help Your Career

1. Searchability. Writers who are hoping their publications in literary journals will eventually lead them to bigger and better things are writers who are hoping to build a platform (a position of influence among a group of fans). Editors, agents, and industry professionals (not to mention friends and family) will Google you if they are interested in your work. You'll want to have something to show them.

2. Connecting with readers via your website or social media. When your writing is published in an online lit mag, it's easy for you to create a centralized directory of your work that is more accessible to readers. On your author website or social media profiles, list your publications with links to the appropriate magazines (or directly to your published writing). If you are published ONLY in print magazines, you cannot create an interactive resource, and readers will find it more difficult to acquire and read your work.

3. Circulation/Print runs. Mid-level print magazines reach an average of a few hundred subscribers. Online publications, however, are not restricted by printing fees and can, therefore, reach a larger audience.

4. Longevity. Poems and stories that are published on the Internet are generally available online for a very long time. Literary magazines will often archive their older editions. For that reason, your online publications will be a resource that you can direct readers to indefinitely. But your old print publications lose their potential to reach new readers when they start to collect dust on your shelf.

5. Online submissions. When you submit to an online literary magazine, you don't have to pay for paper and postage. And you can even make your submissions in your pajamas by submitting your writing to editors and agents via email or via a submission manager (an online form provided by a literary journal that lets you upload and track your submissions).

How To Find The Literary Journals That Are Best For You

We at Writer's Relief are constantly updating our database with information on over a thousand literary magazines and literary agents so we know how difficult and time-consuming the research can be! We cross-check our information using public sources (websites, market books, guidelines, etc.), AND we keep track of editors' and agents' individual preferences based on their personal notes to our clients.

If you're a do-it-yourself type of person, here is what you'll need to know to research the best editors of literary journals.

Market books. These large paperback books are a good place to start if you want to research literary journals. Market books include thousands of listings of publication outlets, including literary journals and magazines. The most popular are *Writer's Market, Poet's Market,* and *Novel & Short Story Writer's Market.* These books contain a wealth of information that will be useful in your search.

Literary market websites. Many print market books have corresponding online websites that can help you with your search for publications. Just know that sifting through market websites can be time-consuming. Prepare for hard work! You can also go to a website like NewPages, which offers a list of magazines. Our own website offers great lists and ideas too.

Literary magazine websites. Go right to the source: Most literary magazines have websites with guidelines easily available. Plus, many websites will allow you to submit your writing online. Use your favorite search engine to search topics and themes for literary journals: like, *feminist literary journals* or *nature literary journals.*

Online submission websites. Websites like Duotrope help authors find journals and track their submissions. However, they have their drawbacks, which we will address in the next section.

Visit a bookstore. Some bookstores do stock literary journals; check out your local book seller to see if any lit mags are available for sale.

One Big Warning About Lit Mag Research

Market guides are great for general perusing of potential markets. But when it's time to actually submit, you'll need to do some deeper research. Whatever research tool you choose to use, it's important that you cross-check your sources. Many times, these resources list contradictory information. Literary journals' submission guidelines change regularly, and that means supplementary materials are often quickly outdated.

The only way to be sure the information is accurate is to *go directly to the literary journal website and use that information only.*

Also, you'll want to organize your research to prevent yourself from accidentally redoubling your efforts later down the line.

How To Organize Your Literary Journal Research

If there's one thing we've learned in over twenty years, it's that organization is KEY to a good submission strategy. A little effort in the beginning of your search for literary journals will pay off in the long run.

In terms of general lit mag research, here's what you'll want to track:

- Which journals are your favorites and which seem to be the best fit for any given piece
- The reading dates of literary journals (especially your favorites)
- Which journals are NOT your favorites so that you don't waste your time considering them again
- Which journals might work for you someday but not now

At Writer's Relief we track all of these elements—and many more—on behalf of our clients. If you're working on your own, consider these strategies:

If You're Using A Hardcopy Market Book...

Don't be afraid to write in it. We know, we know. Some writers don't like to write in books. When you're researching lit mags, make an exception.

For the literary journals that you know you'll probably *never* submit to, use a red pen to put a small X near the name in the margins. Don't cross out the whole thing; you might change your mind later.

For publications on your "maybe" list, use a yellow question mark. Your favorites can be marked with a green star, but also with sticky notes so that you can turn to those listings quickly.

If a literary journal emails a specific note to you, such as "we don't like second-person narratives," write that in your book. We've been cataloging this type of information based on our clients' feedback for many years; it helps to have an idea of the editors' specific tastes.

If You're Using An Online Database...

You might consider making an Excel or Word file to sort your favorites, maybes, and no ways.

Copy and paste the literary journal's URLs directly into the spreadsheet file—but remember that URLs can always change. When possible, we recommend that you sort using the URL of the literary journal itself, not of the literary journal's listing in the online database.

If You're Using A Submission Tracking Site

Duotrope is a website for writers who are making submissions. You can use it to research literary journals and also to track your submissions. As with any submission system, it has its share of pros and cons. If you have the time, focus, and long-term motivation it takes to make effective submissions, Duotrope may be worth considering.

But keep an eye out for misinformation. Be wary of unreliable statistics about publication and acceptance rates. Always go directly to the literary journal in question. Read all submission guidelines.

We also recommend you have a backup to track your online submissions, when possible. The website is generally reliable, but there's always some danger when you're putting all your eggs in one basket. Here, we give our clients 24/7 access to a detailed chart of their submission history. And we keep backups too.

Use An Organizational System That's Motivating

If you're going to organize, do it in a way that isn't going to frustrate you. If you create a system of organization that's complicated or confusing, chances are you'll make an effort in the beginning, then lose interest. And when you lose interest, you don't get published.

We always keep our clients on track with their writing and submitting; it's one of our most important jobs. You'll need to find a way to stay motivated to make your submission strategy work. A good organization system can help with that.

If You Don't Want To Do The Research Yourself

You can try the "hunt and peck" approach to researching literary journals by using online literary journal databases and lists. Many writers have had success with this method. But know that it IS going to be time-consuming and a lot of work.

At Writer's Relief, we can do all the literary journal research for you: You just write. Learn more about our market research and precision targeting process by visiting our website.

How To Determine If A Literary Journal Is Right For You

Our clients sometimes ask: *How exactly do you determine the quality and reputation of a literary journal?*

While we can't give away our secret formula (our targeting method is part of what makes our program so effective!), we can certainly offer some advice for judging a literary journal so you can determine if it's worth submitting to. You'll also be able to determine if a given journal would be a strong or weak publication credit for you.

Here are some elements that we at Writer's Relief take into consideration when ranking a journal. We would never look at one single element alone when deciding how strong a journal is or where to submit a client's work. It's important to look at all the elements together, including the particulars of a client's writing (level and style), aspirations, publishing history, and practical needs.

Quality of work. Look for high-quality writing. Also, scan for the names of familiar and established writers. If well-known writers are publishing in a particular literary magazine, the publication is probably reputable. If you don't recognize the names of any writers, research a few online. At Writer's Relief, we keep track of which journals are publishing well-known or mid-level writers, or which are mostly publishing unknown or unpublished, first-time writers.

Longevity. We look at how long a journal has been around. Well-established journals that have been publishing quality work by top-tier writers for a very long time are sometimes difficult to get into. That said, we never disregard journals—new or old—that are performing a quality service for the literary community.

Masthead information. Look to see who is editing the journal. If you research the editors online, do you find the biographies of well-published writers? The more experienced the editor, the more likely the lit journal is reputable.

Nominations and awards. Literary magazines must meet certain criteria to nominate their writers for awards like the Best New American series, Best of the Web/Net anthologies, and The Pushcart Prize. Whether or not a magazine makes such nominations factors into our evaluation.

Issue format. How does the overall presentation look? Is it professional, clean, and error-free? Is the layout mediocre? Or poor? Are there a lot of ads? We track all of these elements.

Calendar of publications. We consider the journal's past publication schedule. Is it consistent? Slightly inconsistent? Very inconsistent? We also consider any upcoming issues and publications.

Reputable affiliations. We track all journal affiliates such as colleges, universities, organizations, etc.—and if a journal has no affiliates, we track that too!

Governing organizations. If the literary magazine is a publication of a specific writing group that publishes only the work of its own members, then it's probably not a widely known literary publication.

Submission guidelines. We note who wants what and how they want it. When you consider how many journals exist, it's a huge job. Guidelines must be crystal clear and aboveboard, or we will not recommend the journal to our clients.

* * *

With online literary journals, there are some key differences: Starting a website can be inexpensive and simple, so online literary journals can pop up one day and be gone the next. Of course, there *are* many celebrated lit mags that exist only online. The trick is being able to distinguish between solid online journals and those that are less reputable/reliable/respected. It's important to spend additional time making your evaluation of an online literary magazine before you submit.

Parent or former print magazines. If the online literary magazine is an offshoot a reputable journal—or once was available in print, the online literary magazine likely maintains the same quality.

Copyright dates. Don't assume that the existence of a website means that the journals are active. Check for the most recent issue and calls for submissions, or send an email to confirm that the journal is still publishing.

Issue format and layout: Is it a journal or a blog? Editors of reputable online journals will create an issue by linking to the works that are individually posted on the website and/or as a downloadable PDF (free or subscription-based). Be sure all the links go to the right places.

If a website posts one poem or story at a time, it is probably not a true literary magazine; it's a blog. (Note: Blogs dedicated to creative writing should not be dismissed by default. Many reputable literary magazines also have reputable blogs.)

Mission statement. If the mission statement says, "I wanted to create a magazine for my friends and me to showcase our work—oh, and other writers can submit as well," then you are probably not looking at a magazine that is highly reputable in the literary community.

Print editions. Occasionally, online journals will print anthologized editions of their best online publications. If the online magazine is putting out an occasional print publication, it may work in your favor.

Striking A Balance: Where To Submit

So now that you know some of the criteria that must be considered in order to determine the quality of a literary journal, here is the same information presented in a different format. Keep in mind that—again—there are no rules that make one literary journal more prestigious than any other.

The following is not a fine-tuned analysis of how to make evaluations: This is simply a basic guide.

Mid- to upper-end journals

- Often (but not always) university sponsored
- Often (but not always) have some longevity
- Good to excellent writing
- Often but not always perfect bound
- Good to excellent circulation
- May or may not nominate for major awards
- Good to excellent editors

The best of the best

- Very high circulation (rivals commercial magazines)
- Tends to favor established or famous writers (exclusive)
- Long publication history

Casting A Wide Net: Develop A Game Plan For Approaching Literary Journals

Many writers face this internal debate when they start submitting:

> *Should I try submitting right away to the biggest names in the business—but risk excessive rejection?*

—OR—

> *Should I consider starting with lesser-known literary journals—increasing the odds of acceptance but seemingly risking some clout?*

Why You Should Submit To A Range Of Literary Journals

At Writer's Relief, we encourage our clients to submit to a wide variety of journals. In the same way that it's important to list ample work experience on your résumé, submitting to a plethora of journals—and showing off those credits in your cover letter—can demonstrate that your work speaks to a variety of editors and readers.

We understand that many writers dream of being published in *The New Yorker* or the *Paris Review*—after all, doesn't every artist want to be featured at the Louvre?

But it's important to keep in mind that every writer is the new kid on the block at some point in his or her career, and it's sometimes best to build publication credits in midsize literary journals before going after the really big fish.

Work Your Way To The Top One Catch At A Time

One strategy our clients use is to explore (and appreciate) the wide range of journals available. We target our clients' work to an eclectic mix of journals, consisting of both reputable independent presses and bigger-named publications. This helps the writers we work with achieve a higher acceptance rate since their work is viewed by both the "big fish" and the "little fish" too. You can take a similar approach with your submissions.

Making A Case For Midsize Lit Mags

Mid-range journals may not be as well-known as the previously mentioned journals, but they can offer the same, if not more, opportunities for up-and-coming writers. Here's why:

1. Brand-new journals, as well as mid-range journals, are often willing to take risks on publishing new and mid-level writers.

2. Editors at smaller publications are typically available for contact. It is not uncommon for a writer to network or to build a relationship with an editor of a smaller press if they show interest in your work. This can lead to all kinds of advancements and networking opportunities down the road.

3. Many small and midsize literary journals regularly nominate their published writers for *Best New American, Best of the Web, The Pushcart Prize*, etc. So while your publication credit may not have name brand recognition, your nomination certainly could.

4. In the age of digital publishing, many journals gain momentum faster than they used to. Online journals can publish more frequently, reach a wider audience than print journals, and, therefore, accept more work within one publishing year. Just as your reputation as a writer builds over time, newer journals gain fame in their own right. Being published in a lesser-known journal when it's first starting up could hold more clout in the long run!

5. Your midsize publications can be stepping stones toward something bigger. Some editors at the big-name journals may be more interested in your writing if they see you've been published elsewhere. Some unpublished writers DO find themselves at the top of the top with only one or two submissions, but this isn't the norm.

We know that listing super-impressive lit mag publications in your author bio can be great for bragging rights, but we also feel that the best long-term strategy to get those publications is to approach a wide range of literary journals.

A diverse bio is a strong bio—with a mix of nominations, online and print publications, establishing mags, cutting-edge publishers, etc.

Reading Fees And Literary Journals: Your Call

Because we've been helping creative writers since 1994, we've been around to see all the ways that literary journals have changed over the years. In the beginning, most literary journals eschewed any reading fees or monetary charges for authors who wanted to submit.

But more and more, literary journals are beginning to charge fees to writers who make online submissions. In fact, CLMP—the Council of Literary Magazines and Presses, the trade organization for literary journals—hosted a discussion with editors of various literary journals to determine which practices are ethical and which might not be. That way, literary journals affiliated with CLMP can make ethical choices.

It goes without saying that some writers are unwilling to pay fees associated with submissions; some even feel affronted or resentful. But the fact remains that lit mags need to find a way to stay in business, and small reading fees can help.

Here are just a few of the most salient points from CLMP's submission fee discussion that illuminate some of the reasons for the practice.

1. Submission fees should be minimal. Generally speaking, one to three dollars seems to be the accepted submission fee of the moment. An online submission fee of three dollars is often less than what it would cost to mail the same submission by traditional post. So in a sense, making an online submission actually *saves a writer money*—even when there is a fee.

2. It's not a reading fee. While most everyone agrees that reading fees are unethical, literary journals that do charge fees do not charge them as "reading fees." Instead, they are administration fees.

Because so many literary journals have a presence both online and in print, administration fees have gone up. Literary journals that do accept submissions online must maintain websites and databases that make digital submissions possible. This costs them money. But—unlike paper submissions—online submissions don't cost a writer a penny over what they're already paying for their basic Internet.

3. Small fees can translate into more money for writers. The literary journals that are not using the fees to recoup money for the cost of their online submission platform are using them to actually pay their writers

upon publication. Traditionally, the payment for publication in a literary journal is small or nonexistent. Minor fees associated with submissions could help change that.

4. Small fees curtail submissions from writers who aren't taking the process seriously. In the CLMP round table discussion, a representative from *Mid-American Review* talked about a single writer who submitted online and sent seventeen different submissions at the same time. The editor pointed out that if there was a submission fee, it would have been unlikely that this writer would have made so many submissions.

Because it is so easy for writers to submit online, and because it costs nothing, some editors report that some of the submissions they receive are inappropriate. Writers can send off their submissions now much more easily than they could in the past. As a result, editors are inundated by submissions from writers who don't especially care about submission guidelines or editorial preferences. This wastes editors' time. It's also quite disrespectful.

Submission Fees And Literary Journals: Our Thoughts

As we've said, the vast majority of reputable literary journals don't make money. Most are not-for-profit and they are staffed by volunteers. Editors are seeing much-needed financial support decline at universities and colleges.

We think it's fair to say that most writers do not subscribe to every single literary journal to which they submit their work (though, in a perfect world, we know you'd want to!). However, these same writers benefit greatly when a literary journal does accept them for publication.

We cannot take good literary journals for granted. The work they do is important; writers depend on them. In a best-case scenario, the relationship between writers and literary journals would be completely symbiotic—that is, mutually beneficial.

Would you buy an editor a cup of coffee simply to say thanks for all the hard work that he or she does on behalf of the larger writing community? We suspect the answer is yes.

And yet, the editors of journals associated with CLMP are not buying themselves cups of coffee with writers' submission fees. They're creating publication venues for writers. Small administrative fees can help struggling literary journals stay on their feet—and that's good for writers. If a journal's ability to stay viable is dependent upon charging a very small submission fee, then we at Writer's Relief support an ethical practice. We hope you will too.

Part Two

The Submission Process

Strategies And Etiquette For Making Successful
Submissions To Literary Journals

Let's Start With A Little Lingo

Before we can talk shop, it is imperative that you know the language of publishing.

Here is a list of commonly used (and confused) terms in the publishing business:

What is an SASE? A Self-Addressed Stamped Envelope sent with a snail mail submission for the return of an editor's response.

What does previously published mean? As online publishing increases, the term "previously published" becomes increasingly murky. We're going to dedicate a lot of time to this term later, but for now, here's the short answer: If the work has been made available to the public in any way, it's considered previously published.

What is media rate at the post office? Media rate can be applied to mailing packages containing books, scripts, sound recordings, video tapes, and computer-readable media (such as CDs, DVDs, and flash drives). Media rate is slower and less expensive than first-class mail.

What are simultaneous submissions? When you make a simultaneous submission, you send the same submission to more than one literary magazine at the same time.

What are multiple submissions? When you make a multiple submission, you send many submissions (a story and a group of poems) in one envelope or email to one editor.

What is a literary agent? A professional who agrees to represent a book and send to publishers and ensures the best deals for their clients.

What is an editor? An editor works at a publishing house or literary journal. An editor reads submissions, acquires the rights to publish them (sometimes paying for that right), and often edits the content. People who acquire short works for inclusion in a collection or anthology are also editors.

What is a proofreader? Proofreaders edit your work for grammar, punctuation, spelling, and formatting.

What is a copyeditor? A copyeditor edits a manuscript to meet the house style, which includes reading for accuracy and formatting.

What is an exclusive read? If you grant an exclusive read (or right of first refusal), you are granting the right to read your work before anyone else. This rarely happens with lit mag editors but often happens with literary agents.

What are galleys? A galley is an unformatted, not-quite-finished version of a publication.

What is the slush pile? A slush pile is a stack of unsolicited submissions to book agents, literary journals, or publishing houses.

What are solicited and unsolicited submissions? A solicited submission is work that an editor or literary agent has asked for. An unsolicited submission is work that an editor or literary agent has not asked for.

What is an advance on a book or novel? An advance is payment a publisher gives a writer for a book or novel before it is written.

What is a writer's backlist? A writer's backlist is a list of his or her older publications; the term commonly refers to books.

Do New, Unpublished Writers Have A Shot At Being Published?

If you've been in the creative writing world long enough, you've probably heard a writer lament, "In order to get published, you have to be published already!" And yet, if having publishing credentials in order to get published was truly necessary, no one would be published at all.

There are many publishers, presses, literary magazines, and publishing houses that acquire the books, short stories, poems, and novels of new, unpublished writers. It's just a matter of being at the top of your game and knowing where to look.

Local Papers, Private Publications, and Specialty Publications

While having your work published in a small, monthly hometown paper (whose editor was at your barbecue last year) might not be the most glamorous publishing credential, smaller publications in your region are a great place to start. Often, editors of local magazines, e-zines, and community newsletters are thrilled to print the work of up-and-coming writers from their area.

If you want to tap into this market, be sure you're the right person to do it: If you're not truly enthusiastic about participating in your community with like-minded readers and writers, you might not be a prime candidate for this type of publication.

You might also consider writing for a specialty newsletter. For example, many corporations, religious organizations, and clubs issue community bulletins and newsletters on a regular basis. Why not see about getting your writing published there? Or learn if there are any local magazines targeted to a specific audience. Many locales will have smaller poetry magazines or periodicals about nature, education, or local living. Those are great venues for new writers.

Online Literary Magazines

New writers would do well to take the booming world of online literary journals very seriously. A writer's online presence (and online platform) has become increasingly important. Ignore online journals, and you ignore an important aspect of getting your work published.

Because online journals don't typically have the same kind of operating costs as print literary magazines, they do have a little more leeway to take a risk on a new writer. Choose your online journal submissions carefully, and you could end up with a fantastic portfolio.

Print Literary Magazines And Journals

Print literary journals DO frequently publish work by new writers. At Writer's Relief we've been helping writers submit their work to literary magazines since 1994—and we're not going to tell you that it's *easy* to be accepted for publication in a reputable print magazine. But it is possible.

Here's a fun story: Once, a client came to us totally unpublished and with no formal training. We helped place that client's first short story in a literary journal—and of course we celebrated with him! A first publication is a big deal. But then, the client went on to earn a nomination for the *Best New American* series—in and of itself, this is a huge accolade. Will you be surprised to hear that the client's work was ultimately selected for inclusion in the published anthology? All that for a writer who had never published anything before.

So new writers ARE being published in lit mags. We see it *all the time.* It is possible. And we regret when we hear bitterness creeping into a writer's tone when he or she repeats the old chestnut about having to be published to get published. A negative outlook is rarely part of a successful submission strategy.

Literary magazine editors are always on the lookout for exciting new writers. And to many editors, your writing background matters very little. It's the quality of the writing that dictates whether you'll get published—that, and how well you researched your journal selections.

Your Step-By-Step Guide To The Submission Process

If you want to be published in a literary journal, here are the basic steps you'll need to take. Through the course of this book, we'll continue to examine in detail these various elements of a strong submission strategy. But for now, here's the breakdown:

1. Write well.

2. Know the market. Are you reading literary journals? Do you know what you're up against? Make reading one of the most important parts of your journey toward publication.

3. Proofread and format. Does your manuscript meet industry standards? Is it error-free? Find a professional proofreader to help; you can always give us a call or send us an email. (We'll address this in the next section.)

4. Write your cover letter. (We'll give you some pointers on how to write a great cover letter in a later section.)

5. Research, research, research. Researching can take countless hours, but it's a vital and necessary part of making submissions that get results.

6. Mail or email your submissions, and track where and when they go out.

7. Track your responses. Keep track of acceptances, rejections, and any personal notes that may
be helpful in the future when you submit again.

8. Wait. Sometimes it can take a long time to hear back from literary journals.

9. Rinse and repeat!

If Those Are The Steps, What's the Plan?

Some writers make submissions in spurts—a few here, a few months rest, a few more, then quitting again.

You can take an unmethodical approach, hopping on and off the submission highway as you please. But we recommend a more deliberate and goal-oriented method.

We've heard too many stories about writers who start out with lots of enthusiasm for making submissions, only to quit over time. It's one thing to understand the steps necessary to make smart submissions, but it's another thing to actually do it regularly.

Perfect Your Personal Proofreading

No matter what you're submitting to an editor or agent—whether it's a book, story, or just a query/cover letter—one of the most important things you'll need to do is proofread. Time and again we've heard industry professionals lament the lack of proofreading in otherwise good submissions. Don't make the mistake of thinking you can rely on someone else to proofread for you later down the line!

It can be extremely difficult to proofread your own writing. In a perfect world, your letters and submissions should be proofread by a third party who has professional expertise in working with creative writers. At Writer's Relief, we offer proofreading and formatting services to writers of books, novels, stories, poems, and essays. We must turn away about 99% of the proofreaders who apply to work with us; we caution you not to underestimate the difficulty of truly good proofing. When possible, seek expert help.

That said, not everyone can afford a professional proofreader who can put the finishing touches on a submission. If you are self-proofing, the first thing you must do is become an expert on grammar, usage, punctuation, spelling, etc. Once you feel that you have strong proofreading skills that you could apply to someone else's work, take these steps to make sure that you can proof your own work as well.

1. Proof your work both electronically AND by hard copy. Why both? Electronically, you can spot formatting errors and use the spell-check function. And it's easier to read a printout than to read from the computer screen, thereby catching those errors that the eye is most likely to skip over.

2. Choose a time of day when you're most alert and fresh. Take a hard copy of your work and a red pen or pencil, and read through one time, word for word. Run a pen or your finger along as you go to avoid skipping two-letter words and to avoid skipping from one obvious error to the next and ignoring the words between. Make corrections or notations as you go.

3. Bear in mind your own most common mistakes and then proofread for those specific errors. For example, if you have difficulty with comma placement, proof for punctuation only. Then proof again, concentrating on another troublesome area, such as run-on sentences or dialogue. If

you're not sure of your own trouble areas, have someone else read your work and flag the most common errors.

4. Check boilerplate text, headers, footers, and text in tiny font—all areas that tend to get skipped over.

5. Be prepared to look it up. Use a standard dictionary (*Merriam-Webster*, for example) and double-check hyphenated words (non-existent or nonexistent?) and the correct spelling of foreign places or historical figures; the Internet is a great tool for looking up brand names (Jell-O), pop culture references, or song lyrics.

6. Proofread electronically by running your spell-check program. Although the spelling function is fallible (it won't always flag "form" as incorrect if you meant to use "from"), it does catch misspellings that the eye often can't.

7. Check for formatting errors. Turn on the "view ¶" function to check for spacing, indents, etc. Check the margins. You can use the find and replace function to find mistakes that are likely made repeatedly. (Search for "it" if you want to check for "its" versus "it's" throughout.)

8. Be sure to take breaks between steps, giving your eyes a fresh perspective each pass through.

9. Read your work aloud. This forces you to slow down and hear the difference between what you wrote and what you meant to write.

If you would like to learn more about Writer's Relief's proofreading and formatting services, please visit our website. In the meantime, good luck with your own proofing!

So, You Need To Write A Strong Cover Letter

There is no real "magic" to writing cover letters to literary editors. There are four basic elements that you need, and that's it! We'll break it down for you.

1. SALUTATION

You should not assume the gender of the reader of your cover letter, no matter how certain you may be that Lu and Pat are females. And it's not acceptable to contact a literary editor and ask, "Are you a female or male?"

In order to avoid embarrassment and alienating an editor, follow what have now become industry standard rules for addressing these decision makers.

Simply use the first and last name of the editor to whom you are sending your submission, without a Mr. or Mrs. salutation (example: Dear Pat Doe). This technique is sometimes used for mass mailings, but because it is useful and gender-neutral, it has now become standard business protocol for professional correspondence.

Using both names for your submissions won't be held against you. But if you address an editor by the wrong gender, you're starting off on the wrong foot.

2. INTRODUCTION TO WHAT'S BEING SUBMITTED

In one sentence, let the editor know what you're submitting. Here are some examples:

I am submitting my short story, "The Marriage," for your consideration.

For poetry, you can choose how to organize your titles:

Please consider my poems: *Fishing, On The Old Cliffs, Mr. Shriner's Dog,* and *Marking Time.*

Or

Please consider my poems:

"Fishing"
"On The Old Cliffs"
"Mr. Shriner's Dog"
"Marking Time"

NOTE: You do not need to include a description about your poems, short story, or essay. By doing so implies that the editor is not intelligent enough to figure out the plot and themes on his or her own.

3. AUTHOR BIO/PUBLICATION CREDITS

These days, editors are looking for shorter bios (anywhere from 150–300 words). Your bio should be written in first or third person, depending on the journal's guidelines, and should showcase your publication credits (list the top five, for example), any well-known and reputable contests you've won or were a finalist/honorable mention, or any interesting hobbies or work that you do that will make you stand out as a person. Don't worry if you're new to the submission process; every editor knows a writer has to start somewhere.

4. CLOSING LINES

Thank the editor for his or her time and consideration. If you are submitting in hard copy, make a note that you have included an SASE. Editors will know whether or not you want your work returned by the size of the envelope and the amount of postage.

NOTE: Your letter should be written in the same font as your work—most likely in Times New Roman or Arial 12-point font.

Take a look at our website for other cover letter writing tips!

How To Make The Writer's Relief Method Your Own

You know we've been helping writers make and manage submissions for over twenty years. Our system works: It keeps our clients writing and submitting (and getting acceptances). We've seen the incredible power of combining a reliable calendar of goals with the somewhat less reliable nature of creativity: there's balance and effectiveness when the two meet.

So we're going to tell you how *our* system works for our clients. Then, you can try putting it to good use on your own.

Step 1: Research, research, research. We'll say it again—when you're submitting to lit mags, you're going to have to do a lot of research. Sending the right submission to the wrong journal is a recipe for rejection.

Unfortunately, this part of the Writer's Relief system will be hard to replicate on your own: Our submission strategists monitor thousands of markets that are updated anytime there's a change with a literary journal or agent. We've got a team of people constantly working on keeping up to date on new markets and submission guidelines.

For your own DIY submission method, we recommend starting by identifying 25 markets that you like (and saving your notes in a secure place so that you can refer back to them later should you ever want to make more submissions).

Step 2: Set goals for creating new work. Here, our clients submit new work once every two months (our book authors often submit short pieces to literary journals while they are looking for a literary agent, so that they can continue to build up their author bios). How often do you think you can create new work? We recommend trying to write and submit a new story, a new essay, or a new group of poems once every 60 days.

Step 3: Set goals for getting your submissions "out the door." We've previously stated that our clients strive to create new work once every two months. (Sometimes, they don't—and that's fine. It happens.) When it's time to submit their new work, we suggest at least 25 markets for one "round" of submissions.

You might want to target ten lit mags in one round. Or maybe just three. But here's the truth based on our experience: Successful submissions can be a numbers game. We recommend that our clients don't "quit" on a piece until it's been read by 100 markets. For that reason, we make 25 submissions per round.

If you decide to create a new work (or 3–5 poems) once every two months, you can block off seven of those eight weeks strictly for your writing. Then use the last week as a "research and submit week," when you focus on sending your writing to editors.

Step 4: Diligently track submissions and responses. We use an amazing, custom, complex database to track every element of a submission and response. You can do the same thing by creating your own tracking system in Excel. We recommend that you have the following column headings:

- Journal Name
- Poetry Group/Story Title
- Date Sent
- Date Responded
- Any Comments?
- Website

Step 5: Repeat regularly. Once your submissions have been sent to journals, it's time to emotionally let them go. Whatever happens, happens. The only thing you can do to move forward is to keep writing. Then, when your designated "research and submit week" rolls around, you'll be able to move into new territory and improve your odds of getting an acceptance letter by sending more work out into the world.

Whatever goals you decide on, stick to them. Create a submission strategy calendar/schedule for yourself, and celebrate when you begin to reach your publication goals!

What Is Considered Previously Published Writing?

Now that we've talked about methods for developing a personal submission strategy, we have to delve into some specifics regarding making submissions. And we're going to start with a tricky topic: previously published writing.

It is common practice for literary journals to reject previously published writing. Many refuse to even consider it.

Most literary journals don't want previously published poems, stories, or essays because editors want to ensure that their publications are new and unique. In other words, editors want to be first to discover your writing. Also, editors would prefer to stay away from any rights entanglements.

But what exactly does previously published mean?

The answer to this question has become increasingly hard to pin down.

The Definition Of Previously Published:

Back when print publishing was the sole option for sharing work, previously published was an easily defined term. If your poems, stories, or essays appeared in a book, journal, anthology, textbook, newsletter, newspaper, magazine, or any other publication, your work was considered published. If it didn't, it wasn't. Simple. But now, more complicated questions arise.

Is Work Considered Previously Published If I Post It On A Blog, Website, Large Social-Networking Site, Or Online Literary Journal?

If you've posted your writing on any of the above sites, it *is* generally considered previously published.

Is My Work Considered Previously Published If I Post It In A Writing Forum Or Web Board?

If the forum or Web board is *private* and intended for the purposes of encouraging feedback or community support from a small group, then most editors and literary agents will consider the work unpublished. But just in case, you may want to take it down once you've received feedback so it doesn't appear online.

If the forum in question is public (that is, if nonmembers can see what you've written), then your work will likely be considered previously published.

What If I Published My Work On My Blog Or Other Website, But Then I Take It Down Before Submitting It—Is That Considered Previously Published?

This can be tricky. Try not to publish your work online if you plan to submit it elsewhere (like print journals). If you did post online, no one can stop you from taking your work down and then submitting it, but be warned: Editors may not like this tactic.

Once your work is removed from the Internet, do a search of random lines from the work to make sure it is not appearing anywhere. Google and other search engines often archive old Web pages, so simply deleting your work from the Web doesn't mean it's gone! If an editor finds your "unpublished" work online, you might look irresponsible or, worse, devious.

If I Publish An Excerpt Online, Does That Mean The Whole Work Or Part Of The Work Is Considered Previously Published?

Generally speaking, excerpts are okay to publish online, as long as they are on the short side (relative to the work in question).

What if I Self-Published A Book, Then I Want To Submit A Small Piece Of The Book To Lit Mags As A Short Story. Is That Story Considered Previously Published?

Again, if it's available to the public, it's considered published. Most editors would consider the story to be published.

Previously Published Novels And Books

The rules for determining what is previously published change when you move into the book-publishing business. We're including this information for your future reference, even though it doesn't directly pertain to lit mags. File this under "good to know."

Literary agents and publishers at traditional publishing houses have different expectations and goals than editors of literary magazines, so the concept of what it means to be previously published can shift.

The laws (and the industry jargon) are still trying to catch up to the technology. Keep in mind that the following points are general guidelines: Each literary agent or editor may have his or her own definition of what is considered previously published.

Is A Hard Copy Self-Published Book Considered Previously Published For The Purpose Of Finding A Literary Agent?

What this question asks is: "Can I pitch my self-published book to literary agents?" If you've published a book or novel on your own or with a third-party POD publishing company, and you still retain the copyright, you can pitch it to most literary agents. That said, always be forthcoming about your book's history.

Is A Self-Published Book Offered In Electronic Format Considered Previously Published?

The majority of literary agents are willing to consider a book that has been published electronically (published in a digital, nonprint format) as long as the author holds all rights. However, you may need to remove your book from online bookstores and take your book down from the Internet.

If I Publish An Excerpt From My Book Online Or In Print, Does That Mean The Work Is Considered Previously Published?

Generally speaking, it's okay to publish excerpts online, as long as they are on the short side (relative to the book in question). Be sure you maintain the copyright if you're going to publish a portion of your book prior to publishing the whole thing! Otherwise you could end up publishing your book, minus your previously published first chapter!

The Flip Side: Publishing Your Work Online Can Be Beneficial

The Internet can be a wonderful resource, especially for those who don't have critique groups or workshops available in their area. Unfortunately, very talented writers who just happened to workshop their writing online are getting caught in the cross fire between editors, agents, and the rapidly evolving question of "What is previously published writing?"

There are journal editors and literary agents who don't really care about work published on small websites. Did you put a story up on a message board for critique? Have you posted a chapter of your manuscript on your blog? As long as the work isn't plagiarized from someone else, some literary agents and editors don't mind if the writing has appeared online.

But until the industry fully adjusts to the presence of the Internet, many editors are going to simply reject writing they consider to be previously published. At this point, the best option for authors is to play it safe until the rules become clearer.

As a general rule of thumb: If you plan to submit your work to long-established literary journals and magazines or to literary agents and editors, DON'T post it publicly online first.

Lit Mag Contests: How To Know If Submitting To A Writing Contest Is Worth Your Time

If you're submitting to literary journals, you might want to consider submitting to contests too.

Many literary journals, schools, and private individuals host writing contests. If you've spent some time entering writing contests, you know they are an investment. Most contests charge entry fees. Plus, there's the "cost" of your time. And when you don't win, you may begin to think, "Well, that was twenty dollars down the drain!"

But writing contests CAN help your career if you play your cards right. Having diverse writing credentials is important if you're trying to establish a reputation. A mix of publications, awards, nominations, and even a few contest wins can go a long way.

At Writer's Relief, we recommend that our clients (and all writers) enter contests. But how does a writer know when the entry fee and time spent are worth it?

Here are the questions you'll need to ask yourself before you hand over your entry fee:

1. Is this contest reputable?

First things first: Don't enter shady contests. Look for contests that have a solid reputation and longevity (contests that have been running for several years or even decades).

2. Who are the sponsors and organizers?

If the contest in question is run by a well-known lit mag, then you know you're looking at a contest of great renown. If the contest in question is run by Sam's Auto Club and Horseshoe Factory, you're probably not looking at a contest that is well-known in the industry.

If you can't find the information you need from the "About Us" section of the contest's website, email the organizers and ask for details.

3. Who are the judges?

Often, it's the judge who can make or break a contest's reputation. Some organizations don't disclose judges (often, literary journal contests are simply judged by the journal's editors, with no special mention of specific judges).

But a specific judge of a contest might affect your willingness to enter. If a new contest—one that nobody has heard of—is being judged by a fantastic, famous author, you might want to enter. If you win, you can say "*Mr. Famous* selected my story to win the *You've Never Heard Of This Contest Prize.*" The famous author's name goes a long way toward recognition and bragging rights.

4. What's the relationship of the payment and the payout?

Would you pay ten bucks for a shot at being published in your favorite magazine, with the added incentive of a cash prize, a subscription, and/or the good karma points of financially supporting a publication you admire? If so, then this contest is probably a GO for you.

Would you pay ten bucks so an unknown editor can consider publishing your work on his or her unknown website (which means said work will then be considered previously published and, therefore, less likely to be eligible for publication elsewhere)?

Maybe, maybe not. Read on.

5. Would winning this contest positively augment your current writing credentials?

If you are a Pulitzer winner, entering a contest that Joe American runs out of his home office isn't going to help much. Sure, you might win. Just like a shark might win a fight with a goldfish. But would winning increase your reputation or credentials? No.

But if you've never published anything before, then winning a smaller contest could be a windfall! There are some ethical but lesser-known contests out there that are really fantastic for newer writers. In fact, some contests are specifically created to encourage aspiring writers.

Look honestly at your publication credits and see if a win would be a step forward for you. If winning the contest means you'll go from being just another goldfish in the school to being the goldfish at the head of the class, then proceed to enter.

6. Who will your competition be?

Certain contests—the well-known, respected contests—attract high-level, professional writers (Hint: These are the contests you should really want to win). Other contests attract hobbyists and new writers. Often, you can determine this by looking at the judges, affiliates, and lists of writers who have won in the past.

Keep in mind that there is no rule that says you can't email a writing contest organizer and ask, "How many entries did you receive the last time you ran this contest?" You might not get an answer, but it doesn't hurt to ask.

Anthologies: More Great Opportunities For Submissions

Anthologies are collections of writings by many authors based on a given theme. Literary journals often publish themed issues that could be considered anthologies.

An anthology gathers stories and/or essays that center around a common theme, which opens up a great avenue for aspiring authors. Are you a lifetime hiker? There's probably an anthology of nature-based tales waiting for your contribution. Are you a cancer survivor? Caretaker of an elderly parent? If there's a common thread that makes people feel a connection with each other, there's likely a market for your story. These publications depend on the contributions of folks just like you.

Whether you submit to an independent anthology or to a themed literary journal, you're on the trail of a great opportunity!

Anthologies are rich with possibilities for new writers hoping to be published. And they're a popular market now—simply count the number of *Chicken Soup for the Soul* collections in circulation.

Editors of anthologies frequently put out calls for submissions from new and established writers. Anthologies are often started as a way to fill gaps in the market when a publishing house perceives a need for a certain theme. Sometimes authors get together and submit samples as an anthology package, other times a single author comes up with the idea and invites other writers to submit.

A few things to look out for when choosing to submit to an anthology:

1. Check the simultaneous submission policies so that you can circulate your work to more than one potential anthology or literary journal.

2. You should not be forced to purchase the anthology that has published your work, and you should receive at least one free copy plus discounts on additional copies.

3. If you're going to be paid, get the terms of your payment up front and in writing. Some anthologies pay token fees (which can be acceptable when you consider a great writing credit), while others pay quite handsomely.

Overall, anthologies are a great way to get started in this difficult industry. Even if you don't land a lucrative sale, you'll still have a publishing credit, and that is your ultimate goal—getting your work out there to be read.

How To Interpret Submission Guidelines

Whether you're submitting directly to a literary journal, to an anthology, or to any other call for submission, you're going to need to know about the language of submission guidelines.

Submission guidelines have their own industry-specific terms; we'll get you started.

Definitions And Explanations Of Words You'll Find On Submission Guidelines Pages

Book reviews – Some literary journals accept reviews of books, usually of the scholarly or literary variety. However, some journals are not open to book reviews from authors without a query first. Be sure to check.

Payment – Journals may pay in: contributor copies (copies for people whose work appears in the issue); honorariums (token payments given to contributors as budgeting allows); or subscriptions (a free subscription to the journal in question).

Reading period – The time frame during which a literary magazine is open to reading submissions. If the magazine reads from about September to May, you may conclude that the magazine is probably affiliated with a university or college and only operates during the school year. If the reading period is all year or one month only, it's more likely that you're looking at an independent publication.

Response time – The time it will take for you to hear back about your submission. The response time varies from one literary journal to the next.

Sample copy – You can often order a sample copy of a literary journal at a discounted rate to see if your work will be a good fit with the editors there. If the journal is an online journal that does not require subscription, you can simply view the most current issue to get a sense of editorial preferences.

Submission manager – An online database that manages and tracks submissions. Submission managers are revolutionizing the way that small literary journals do business. You can see how to use a submission manager by visiting the Writer's Relief website, going to the video tutorials page under "Leads & Tips" in the navigation bar.

Word count, line count, or page count – For prose, most submissions are measured in word count. Use the word count feature in your word processing program to determine an estimate of your word count, and include the estimate on the first page of your manuscript. Some markets will ask for works that are "no more than ten pages," in which case the word count is a bit flexible. However, be sure you submit according to industry-standard format guidelines: 12-point, simple font (like Times New Roman), one-inch margins, normal paragraph spacing—no funny stuff.

Poetry is generally measured in lines or pages; rarely in number of words. To estimate your line count: Don't count the title or any blank lines as "lines." Just count lines of text to get the number of lines in your poem.

Keep An Eye Out For These Phrases

"We do not accept genre fiction…" If a literary journal's guidelines state that it does not accept genre fiction, this means they do not accept work that could be classified among the commercial genres.

"Only previously unpublished work (or writing)." Most literary journals want first rights to a given work, so they do not acquire previously published work.

"Requires exclusivity, the exclusive right to consider the manuscript, no simultaneous submissions, or the right of first refusal." This means the literary journal wants to be the only entity considering the work in question.

15 Tricks To Make Your Life Easy When You Submit Online

Using an online submission form (or submission manager) can be a very effective way to submit your short stories, personal essays, and poetry to literary journals and magazines.

A submission manager is an online form that a writer fills out. The form creates a profile so that the writer can log in at any time to check on the status of a submission or make a change.

There are some very specific things you can do to make your online submissions happen more smoothly, especially if you're using electronic submissions managers.

(Hint: If you haven't already, go and watch the video tutorial on our website that demonstrates how to use an online submission manager!)

Tips For Making Electronic Submissions To Literary Journals And Magazines

1. Keep a record of which journals and editors you submitted to, the submission method you used, and your user name/email address and password. Save this information where you can refer to it easily. You'll save yourself a lot of time and frustration later on when you're trying to remember where you sent your work.

2. Use the same password each time so you don't have too many to remember. But don't use a password that you share with banks or email accounts or any other websites. Make one up specifically for your writing.

3. Create a new email address to use just for your electronic submissions or make folders in your current email account for sorting your acceptances and rejections.

4. Make sure you read each literary journal's submission guidelines carefully *before* you upload your manuscript! For example, some literary journals do not want your name to appear on your work.

5. Make sure the contact information you have for each market is up to date. Literary journals are picky about their online forms and submission managers, and they are likely to change their preferences from time to

time. (This could be the case if you find their usual submission link fails to load.)

6. Submit to a group of journals that use Submittable (a specific online submission manager used by many lit mags). If you create an account with one journal that uses it, you can use the same account for every journal that uses it. You'll also remain logged in to your account if you have cookies enabled on your computer. This will make it easy to fill out forms!

7. Have your cover letter or professional writing bio ready, because you'll be copying and pasting it into each submission. And remove any references to enclosures or attachments. You won't be including an SASE with an electronic submission.

8. If you're submitting a group of poems, keep a list of all the titles handy; you can copy and paste that into the forms and submission managers. Also, combine all of your poems into one file/document (copy and paste them) because most online forms and submission managers only want one file to be attached.

9. If you goofed on your submission and were using an online form or submission manager, odds are you can log in to your account, withdraw your submission, and resend it. If the "oops" in question was an email submission, you can try resending, but this might annoy editors who don't want duplicate emails. Hooray for submission managers!

10. Double-check your email addresses and URLs. The easiest electronic submission mistake to make is a typo in the email address (or URL).

11. Keep a master electronic file of your work and don't save any changes to it. If you need to tailor your work to a specific journal (i.e., no name on work, single-spaced, no headers or footers, etc.), always save it as a new document. This will save you a lot of time when you want to submit to another journal.

12. Don't save over the master version of your cover letter. (See Tip #11.)

13. You will most likely get an automatic response from an editor stating that they have received your work. Note: This is NOT a rejection. Carefully read your responses to avoid confusion. If the journal emailed you your account information, save this in a designated email folder.

14. Some journals require payment just for sending an electronic submission. We don't discourage you from submitting to those journals; just make sure you include payment so your submission isn't rejected out of hand.

15. Make sure the literary journal is actually accepting the genre of work you are submitting. Sometimes a literary magazine can be closed for poetry but will still accept short stories.

Submitting By Email: Don't Make These Amateur Mistakes

If you're going to submit your work via email (as opposed to a submission manager or online form), be sure to avoid these amateur errors! Consider this your email submissions checklist, and read over it before you hit SEND.

1. No typos. Carefully proofread every email and attachment before sending.

2. Check for slang or lazy abbreviations. Avoid "OMG!" and "What do u think? Pls reply."

3. Get the editor's name right in your salutation. Spell it correctly and play it safe by using his or her full name to avoid embarrassing gender errors.

4. Stick to standard fonts and sizes. Twelve-point Times New Roman and Arial are most common. No funny colors, graphics of smiling bunnies, or oversize signatures.

5. Use the correct spacing. Follow submission guidelines, and use single spacing in your cover letter.

6. Watch for bad formatting. If you've cut and pasted text into an email, send the email to yourself first in order to spot any problems.

7. No rambling. Cover letters should never be more than one page. The same goes for an e-cover letter.

8. No spamming multiple recipients in the same email. Send one email at a time to one journal at a time. Otherwise, your submission will likely be flagged by spam filters. Plus, it's just rude.

9. Don't CC a list of recipients. In any professional correspondence, don't use CC when BCC is appropriate. If you're sending an email to a mailing list or a list of personal industry contacts, don't CC because some recipients may consider it an invasion of privacy.

Remember: Writing an email may seem like a casual and easy effort. But you should approach it as seriously as you would a print submission.

Red Flags That Editors Will Use To Reject Your Submission Fast

Everybody knows the best way to get an acceptance letter is to write well and target submissions well. But did you ever stop to wonder what red flags professional readers look for when they're slogging through piles and piles of manuscripts?

Think of it this way: When you're deciding whether or not you want to eat at a particular restaurant, you're going to glance at the menu quickly before you decide to read further and check out the individual appetizers, entrees, and desserts.

If you're a hardcore carnivore, you're probably going to see the words tofu, tempeh, and seitan as red flags. No need to spend any more time looking at this menu! Let's go to a steak house!

People who are reading submissions (reading them until their eyes blur) also have shortcuts. They look for red flags. They use them as signposts that mean "this might end up being a rejection."

Here at Writer's Relief, we can't accept every writer who wants to join our client list. We reject about 80% of applicants. In order for us to have good relationships with literary journals, our clients' writing must be strong and appropriate for submission. For that reason, writers must apply to join.

Here are the MOST COMMON red flags we see in the submissions that our Review Board (usually but not necessarily *always*) ends up rejecting. We suspect lit mag editors watch for the same red flags when reviewing their submissions.

1. Did not follow submission guidelines. When a writer's submission is way outside of our submission guidelines, he or she may be (inadvertently) proclaiming:

- I don't feel like following guidelines.
- I am not taking this seriously.
- I am not able to follow the directions (this could be for any number of reasons, some of which are legit).

Some red flags are like the little ones that children wave at parades. But blatantly ignoring submission guidelines is a big red flag the size of a parachute. HINT: If you are going to break the rules when making a submission, it may help to explain why you're doing it. Readers are forgiving when they know what to forgive!

2. Formatting. Submit in a simple, common font with your name and page number on each page. The writing should stand out; the formatting should not.

3. Typos. Time and time again, we find typos on the first page of a submission. Even if it's just an out of place comma, those little mistakes are annoying to a reader who still has 90 more submissions to get through. Sure, we'll forgive a stray typo here and there. Nobody's prefect (get it?)! But a reader can only see so many misuses of the word "there" before starting to feel discouraged.

4. The word count isn't suitable for submission. We've had people submit 285,000-word doorstops...er...novels, 10,000-word "short stories." Inappropriate word counts are easy-to-spot red flags.

5. Lack of supplemental materials. At Writer's Relief, we like to get a sense of a writer's personality because we need to work closely with our clients. We like to cultivate good energy here in our office, and we prefer to work with writers who are as enthusiastic about what they do as we are about helping them do it.

BUT some writers will skip the bio section. Or they'll write "I'm a writer" and leave it at that. Imagine if you were excited to learn about a writer's goals, interests, and history—but all he or she told you was "I like to write." Already the reader has a negative reaction even before he or she gets to the actual writing.

6. Writers who send us long, bitter diatribes. We see a number of writers who complain about how literary agents won't take them seriously, poetry editors hate rhyming poems, nobody understands, somebody who helped them self-publish a project gave them the runaround and now are entirely to blame for the failure of said project (never mind the writer's allergy to doing research *before* signing a contract).

Such writers wonder why they're getting rejected at every turn. It breaks our hearts. Seriously. We get it; it's a tough business. ALL writers have it tough at some point. But it's the writers who don't consider themselves victims and persevere that succeed.

The Green Light For Red Flags

Sometimes we come across a truly great writer who means well but just makes a few errors when submitting. Or we find a submission that is so compelling, the writer could have submitted in crayon and we wouldn't care. (NOTE: This is an imaginary scenario. We do not accept submissions in crayon—at least not from anyone over the age of three.)

But if you want to increase your chances of getting an acceptance letter consider how editors use shortcuts to weed through submissions, and avoid hoisting your own red flags.

The Hidden Language Of Lit Mag Rejection Letters

Rejection letters from editors of literary journals can be discouraging—especially impersonal, one-line form letters. But rejection is an unavoidable part of the writing process. Creative writers should know how to interpret the information in rejection letters and then use this knowledge to improve their submissions.

First, let's look at the different types of rejection letters:

The Form Letter Rejection

A form letter rejection is easy to spot. This may be a short, generic note that reads something like, "Dear Writer—No thanks." Or "Dear Writer—Please try again."

There's not much to be learned from a blanket rejection letter. But some literary journals do have "tiered" rejection letters: one form for writers they don't want to encourage; one for people who are good writers but who aren't a good fit; one for writers who are invited to submit again.

Some editors who do not use a form will simply send back a handwritten note or email that says something like, "Not for us."

Standard Phrases Used In Rejection Letters From Editors Of Literary Journals:

- Cannot use it/accept it at this time
- Didn't pique my interest
- Didn't strike a chord
- Doesn't meet our needs
- Doesn't fit our plans
- Have to pass on this
- Isn't resonating with me/us
- Isn't something we'd like to pursue
- Not a right fit
- Not exactly what we're looking for
- Not for us
- Not suitable for us
- Not quite right for this publication
- We are not enthusiastic enough about this work
- We are not right for your work

- We recommend you buy/subscribe/read our magazine
- We do not have a place/room for this

...and the list goes on!

If you receive a rejection letter with phrases like those mentioned here, be careful not to misinterpret it. A form letter doesn't mean you sent your writing to the wrong journal or editor. A form letter, no matter what the exact phrasing, is a nice, easy way of saying, *No, thanks.*

The Personal Rejection

When an editor has taken the time to include a comment about your submission, then you know it's a personalized rejection.

Even if the comment is a critique of your work, we recommend you consider resubmitting to any editor who cared enough about your work to offer a personal comment.

Send the editor a thank-you note, and if/when you resubmit, reference the comments from the original rejection.

An Invitation To Resubmit

Some journals always invite writers to submit again—it's part of their form rejection. But others make such an offer more cautiously. At Writer's Relief, we track our clients' rejections and acceptances, so we know when these kinds of comments are boilerplate phrases in a form letter and when they are personalized.

We invite you to submit more in the future.

Do you have anything else we can consider? Please send.

Why, you may wonder, are you being rejected if the writing is so great?

A piece may be rejected simply because the timing is off. Or your project was too similar to something else already in the works. Or the editor might believe you have talent and he or she is looking forward to seeing you develop it.

Either way, send a thank-you note and a new submission (when possible) and follow the guidelines when you do; and again, reference the original comments in your next submission.

Close, But Not Quite

Often, writers get discouraged when they get too many "near misses." But there's a valuable lesson to be learned if you're receiving rejections that imply "close, but not quite."

Take the time to analyze any comments you've received. Is there a common thread (i.e., tired theme, flat characters, weak ending)?

However, when deciding to make revisions based on feedback, think carefully before you start taking every piece of advice thrown your way. Follow your heart and consider the comments thoughtfully—avoid knee-jerk reactions.

For example: If one editor says "you should have written this in first person," you may want to wait to hear if any other editors have the same comment before making such a drastic revision. It's important to trust your instincts.

Keep in mind that what one editor dislikes, another editor might enjoy! But, if you receive multiple comments that critique the same elements, it may be time to revise.

Finally, if you're getting many nice rejections, it may be time to reevaluate your submission strategy. Maybe you're simply not submitting to the right journals.

Why Do Magazine Editors Use Form Letters?

The fact is, editors receive too many submissions to provide a personal comment on each piece. Hence, form letters.

How Should Writers Deal With Rejection Letters?

Writing is a business, and writers must remember that editors have nothing against them personally.

Editors' jobs depend on the choices they make, and if they don't feel the work will resonate with their readers, they don't have time to argue or explain exactly why.

Editors of literary journals have different tastes and interests, which is why writers should learn what they can from rejection letters and then keep submitting to find an editor who will love their work.

The Frazzled Writer's Guide To Staying Sane While Making Submissions

Dear Writer's Relief: Help! I'm drowning in busy! I know I should be making submissions to literary editors, but I just can't find the time and focus to do it while holding down a job, taking care of a family, and improving my writing technique at the same time. Please—somebody—throw me a flotation device!

If You're Feeling Too Frazzled, Here Are Some Tips For Regaining Your Sanity:

1. Breathe. Seriously. When you're all in a tizzy and have a thousand things to do, stop and take three deep breaths. Remind yourself to stay in the present moment. Will yourself to relax. The work ahead of you will be easier to do if you approach it in a state of relaxed confidence.

2. Steal a little peace. When you're feeling overwhelmed, it's important to treat yourself to a little TLC. Tidy up your work space and reduce visual clutter. Light a candle, put on some soft music, and approach the tasks ahead with a calm, peaceful state of mind.

3. Remember, you can only do one thing at a time. In spite of the world's multitasking technologies, you really can only do one thing at a time. So allow yourself to focus on that one thing (in this case, your submissions). Give yourself permission to focus, and allow your determination to take hold.

4. Get visual (and realistic). When you feel frazzled, small tasks start to look enormous. The things you have to do next week feel like they have to be done right now.

So get organized: List all your tasks on sticky notes. You can color-code them based on urgency or group them based on other categories. Then stick them to a wall, stand back, and take a look at the big picture.

Once your projects are on the wall, you can more easily see what's truly urgent, what can be put off, and how much work is really before you. That task that feels like a boulder sitting on your chest might turn out to be a pebble once you take a realistic look at the situation.

5. When in doubt, get help. This may seem like a no-brainer. But so many of us get used to shouldering every burden alone. It can be difficult to admit (to yourself or others) that you need help. It can be even more difficult to ask for it. Don't be afraid to seek the help you need.

How To Stay Motivated To Keep Making Submissions Even When You Want To Quit

Let's say you have developed the perfect submission strategy: You've got a calendar, you've got all the know-how that you need, and you've got some really great writing to submit. If you're like many writers, you'll dive into your new submission strategy with all your enthusiasm and gumption.

But soon, your interest in making submissions begins to fade. You mean to make submissions to journals—but then you just don't.

The fact is this: The best submission strategy in the world is worthless if there is no motivation backing it up. Here are some things you can do to stay focused and enthusiastic when it comes time to implement your personal submission strategy.

Keep your eye on the prize. There are many ways you can stay focused on your dreams: Post inspirational quotes in your home office. Buy yourself a trophy or some other meaningful item, and set it next to your computer to remind yourself that your goal is a real, tangible thing. Do what you can to stay focused on what you want, and you will find you may be more enthusiastic while you are getting there.

Reward yourself for success. If you set goals for yourself (like, "I will make six submissions this week"), then reward yourself when you meet your goals. Just make sure the reward is something that you really want and something that you would not otherwise allow yourself to have. Otherwise, a reward system will not work.

Seek out others who are in the same boat. When you're struggling and striving, talking about your experiences can be a great way to stay motivated. It helps to vent. It helps to compare notes. It helps to commiserate. Find the emotional support that you need to keep going. Hint: You can meet other writers at local writing groups, at writing organizations, or on the Internet.

Don't be too hard on yourself. At some point, everyone drops the ball. Don't hold yourself to unachievable standards. And if you fall off the wagon, you can always climb back on. Just be sure that you don't let negativity hold you back. Leave your mistakes behind you and move forward.

Don't procrastinate. Procrastination can trigger a vicious cycle: You procrastinate because you don't feel like doing the work, then you begin to feel bad you're not doing it, so you procrastinate some more. If you find yourself wanting to procrastinate, remind yourself of your goals. Focus on the end result, not on the work of getting there.

Seek out things that inspire you. Maybe reading books by your favorite author motivates you to work harder. Maybe you like paging through inspirational quotes by creative writers. Or maybe you enjoy going to the bookstore and picking up books that will teach you how to make the most of your own willpower. Go out and find whatever triggers your positivity. A good feeling about your life's work will get you far.

Make Staying Motivated Your #1 Priority If You Want To Create A Successful, Personal Submission Strategy.

If your heart is in the right place and your attitude is good, then your submission strategy is going to be more likely to succeed. You may find that you don't even need to "fight yourself" in order to make your submissions. Approach your time spent making submissions by looking forward to it.

But if you find that researching and preparing your submissions gets you down, and you really struggle with the process of making your submissions due to time constraints or feelings of negativity, then it's probably best to find another way.

It's rare that anything good comes out of negativity. So the most important thing that you can do to create a strong submission strategy is to find a way to feel positive and motivated about what you're doing— even if that means hiring someone else to do the work on your behalf. It's better to feel good and channel all that positive energy into your writing than to feel bad and find yourself falling into a downward spiral of disappointment. Check out our tips in *The Happy Writer: Your Secret Weapon Against Rejection, Dejection, Writer's Block, And The Emotional Pitfalls Of The Writing Life.* Find out more on our website.

Part Three

Everything That Can Go Wrong...

Solutions For Sticky Situations

The Anatomy Of A Literary Journal Contract

The language of literary journal contracts can be confusing. But we're going to break it down and make it very easy to better understand your literary magazine agreement. Before you sign a contract with a literary journal, be sure you understand it!

Grant of rights. The first part of your contract is usually going to discuss what rights you are specifically granting to the literary magazine in question. We'll examine the basic types of literary journal rights agreements you'll need to know about. The following order reflects the frequency in which you'll encounter these terms.

> **FNASR.** In the old days, a writer would traditionally grant "First North American Serial Rights" (FNASR). The term FNASR applies inherently to print publication rights, and some literary journals continue to use the term. But with the influx of the Internet, writers and publishers today need to be more specific. Your contract should specify whether you are granting first North American PRINT rights or first North American ELECTRONIC rights (or both). If you have posted your work anywhere on the Internet for public view, you cannot offer first rights because the work will already be considered published.

> **Exclusive rights.** You grant the right to the publisher to be the only publisher to release the work in the manner designated.

> **Anthology rights.** Some literary journal contracts will acquire not only first rights, but also the rights to publish the work in an anthology anytime later down the line.

> **One-time rights or reprint rights.** If your work has already appeared in public, you can offer one-time rights or reprint rights. This simply indicates to publishers that the work has appeared elsewhere already.

> **Language Rights.** If you offer first North American rights, you authorize the publisher to print in English in North America. But if you offer **First World English Rights**, you give the right to publish the piece anywhere in the world *in English.* Be sure you know what translation rights you're granting and what territories you're allowing your work to be published in.

All rights. If a literary journal asks for all rights, we recommend you consider running away. "All rights" is just what it sounds like, and it essentially locks you into an obligation that could tie up your work with a given publisher indefinitely.

Compensation. Some literary journals are able to pay their contributors. Some will offer copies of the publication in lieu of cash payment.

Timely publication. In a best-case scenario, your contract will indicate when you can expect your piece to be published. The more specific, the better.

Editorial changes. Your contract should prevent editors from making editorial changes without your approval and should also give you the right to review a final galley of the work prior to publication.

Additional copies. You should be able to purchase additional copies of the issues in which your work appears, sometimes at a discount.

Signing Your Literary Journal Contract

Your editor may ask you to submit your contract by standard post mail; others will find it acceptable to receive a signed, scanned copy via email. Be sure you know your editors' preference.

Then, once your contract is signed, make a note on your calendar so that you can keep track of when the issue that features your work should arrive in the mail. If you fail to receive it, you'll know immediately and be able to contract the editor to ask for details.

We recommend a visit to the National Writers Union website to see a sample literary journal contract. Here at Writer's Relief we're not lawyers and we don't give legal advice. So if you have a question about your literary journal contract, speak with an attorney.

6 Dangers Of Literary Journal Contracts

What Does It Mean To Grant Electronic Rights?

You may assume that "electronic rights" means that your work can appear on the literary journal's website. But it could also mean that your work could appear in e-book form. Also, how long will you want your work to appear online? A year? Ten years? Your electronic right grant could mean that your work will appear online with the literary journal forever.

If you think you might want to see it taken down at some point, you'll need to negotiate that with your potential editor. Ask for a clause that would allow the work to be removed from any digital forms upon request. But be aware that your editor might walk away from the deal if he or she doesn't like your terms. This kind of request is unusual and makes life potentially very difficult for an editor down the road.

How Long Will It Take To Be Paid, To Get Published, Or To Receive Your Contributor Copies?

In a best-case scenario, your contract should specify when these important milestones will happen. Many contracts will offer a maximum time frame, such as "writer will be paid not more than three months after publication." If you contract doesn't offer time frames, you can ask for them to be added in.

What Are Grounds For You To Withdraw Your Grant Of Rights Or Terminate The Agreement?

Suppose the publisher decides not to pay you after all. Or three years go by, and you have not seen your poem published in the literary magazine in question. Your contract should protect you and allow you to withdraw your grant of rights under conditions that are not favorable to you.

Be sure that you understand exactly what it takes to terminate the agreement. Most literary journals will require written notice and—possibly—a certain amount of time to remedy the situation before the termination goes into effect.

If you're granting anthology rights, what format or medium will the anthology be published in?

If you are granting anthology rights, be sure that you know whether that anthology is going to be print or digital. If you grant first North American print rights, but you also grant electronic anthology rights, then your work could appear both in print and online.

Are You Sure You Want To Grant "All Rights"?

This bears repeating. If you grant all rights, be prepared to never see your piece published anywhere else ever again. Generally, don't ever give away all rights. The language is too vague and broad.

No Written Contract?

Some literary journals do not offer a written contract. This isn't out of the ordinary. If you are offered publication without a written contract, you may want to create an agreement of some sort so there is no confusion in the future. We'll show you how.

No Written Contract? What To Do If You Are Offered A "Handshake Deal"

Old-school editors and publishers—and even some new e-publishers—have long relied on nothing more than a figurative handshake to seal an agreement with a writer. Short stories, poems, and personal essays are frequently published by editors at literary magazines without a written contract. But what does it mean if you're offered a place in a publication, but you're not offered a formal contract? What rights are you granting if your work is published without a signed agreement?

Print Publishing Without A Written Contract

The traditional print publishing industry has long operated without contracts for smaller, nonpaying publications. In fact, "no contract" publishing agreements happen so frequently that the industry has developed standards for such so-called handshake deals.

Copyright law holds that any publication occurring without a written contract implicitly grants First North American Serial Rights to the publisher for print editions.

After you've granted FNASR, you can't grant them *again* (only one publication can publish your work first). But you can offer one-time rights (or reprint rights) to any subsequent publishers who might be interested in your work.

Our recommendation: If an editor wants to include your poem or short prose in an issue of a literary magazine but does not offer you a contract, you can always offer your own agreement.

If you and your editor share a clear understanding of what's being granted, then no one's feelings should get hurt.

For example:

Thanks so much for your interest in publishing my work! I'm happy to grant FNASR print rights to Magazine Name.

E-Rights Without A Written Contract

Granting rights for print publications is relatively simple. But e-publications can be a little trickier. The problem with granting e-rights is that, frankly, no one is quite sure what the term "e-rights" even means.

The court systems simply haven't tried enough cases to determine e-rights standards yet. All that's entirely certain is that e-rights must be negotiated separately from print rights, so an agreement about print rights does not necessarily include e-rights.

Our recommendation: Again, the point is that you and your editor must be clear with each other about what's being granted. A note to clarify is helpful.

Example:

Thanks for your interest in my poem! I'm granting you the right to be the first to publish my poem in this online issue of Magazine Name.

Seems easy, right?

But it's not. When you grant the right to publish online, you could be giving the okay for that work to appear on the site in perpetuity. The standard for online literary magazines at the moment is that after the issue in which your work appears is released, the issue can then be archived on the site, where it normally remains searchable and readable.

If you don't want your work to appear on a site indefinitely, then you might want to clear that up with your editor. Be aware, though, that the editor might rescind the offer of publication if you can't agree with the magazine's policies.

You might ask the editor:

Is your magazine willing to take my poem off your website if in the future I request that you do so?

Not all editors will agree—after all, you wouldn't ask an editor to remove your poem from a print magazine after a certain period of time, would you?

The Bottom Line

If you're not offered a written contract from an editor who wants to publish your story, poem, or essay in a literary journal, don't panic! You're allowed to ask questions to clarify what's being granted, and you're allowed to disagree. Just be sure that you and the editor are on the same page—with no room for a mix-up—and write your own agreement stating exactly what you're granting.

The 5 Rookie Mistakes Writers Make When Negotiating A Contract

When offered a contract, most writers are on their own. They feel flattered by being offered a contract. They're eager and excited, or they're humbled and grateful.

Because contract negotiations can be so emotionally charged, some writers find it difficult to negotiate well on their own behalf.

Here are the 5 most important points to keep in mind when you're negotiating a writing contract.

5. Don't assume you know everything or that the contract writer knows best. Some writers assume that the lawyer who wrote the contract they're about to sign obviously knows best about the situation. But as a writer, you must be your own advocate.

Remember: Don't let an *If it were important, I would already know it* attitude cloud your judgment. And don't assume the contract writer is looking out for your concerns. When in doubt, hire a literary lawyer who is an expert and who will specifically look out for your best interests.

4. Don't be overly trusting. It's only natural that a writer who is flattered by being offered a contract of any sort might be inclined to trust the person offering the contract. After all, if a publisher is smart enough to see that your writing is worth a contract, doesn't that make them implicitly better and more trustworthy than the editors that didn't offer a contract?

Remember: It's easy to say "I wouldn't think that" when you aren't in that situation. Just be aware that many writers make the mistake of being too trustworthy when entering into an agreement. A healthy amount of caution, even skepticism, is important to your writing career.

If you weren't offered a written contract and were instead offered a handshake deal, remember that it's okay to ask for something in writing.

3. Don't rush and don't allow yourself to be rushed. When you're offered a contract, it's tempting to quickly sign on the dotted line, agree to everything, and give in to the urge to hurry the process along. Add that to the pressure from a publisher to sign the contract now, now, now, and you've got a recipe for disaster.

Remember: You can take your time. Did it take months to write your short story? If so, what's a few days more? Patience in all things related to writing helps.

2. Don't let gratitude turn you into a doormat. Some authors are ignored for years. So when they finally are offered a crumb of attention from an editor, it can be easy to become overly agreeable. This can lead a writer to agree to terms that aren't necessarily in his or her favor.

Remember: You can be grateful and glad without agreeing to everything. If you feel uncomfortable about an element of your contract, discuss it. You and your publisher want the same thing: to come to an agreement that you BOTH can feel comfortable about for a long time. Give your editor the benefit of the doubt, and don't be embarrassed to bring up any terms that make you feel uncomfortable. If you receive an unprofessional or insensitive response, then you'll know it's time to head in a different direction.

1. You have the power in a negotiation. If you've been offered a contract, it's because you hold the rights to a commodity that's desirable. That means the ball's in your court—to an extent.

Editors and publishing professionals who have been in the business for years can be intimidating to a new writer. And intimidation, coupled with intense emotions, can lead a writer down a slippery path.

So take your time, step back, and remember: Nobody but you owns your writing. And nobody can replace you. You are in a unique position, and you deserve to negotiate a contract that works in your favor.

How To Follow Up With A Literary Journal If You Haven't Heard Back

It's hard to be patient when you're making submissions of poetry, essays, and stories to literary journals. But response times vary—anywhere from a few days to over a year. So how (and when) should you follow up with a literary journal that you haven't heard back from?

First, Ask Yourself Why You Are Following Up.

What's your reason for wanting an answer now, as opposed to six months from now? If you have a good reason editors may be more inclined to sympathize with you and prioritize your submission. But unless a very, very long time has passed, the best thing to do is wait. Most literary journal editors work for free or for very little. Many magazines are staffed by volunteers who do the job because they love it. Literary journals serve the writing community in many ways; be patient with them. Hopefully they will return the favor!

What If I Got An Offer Of Publication From One Literary Journal, But I'm Really Hoping To Hear Back From A Different One? Can I Follow Up With My Preferred Journal?

You can, but be careful. Editors tend to stick together and support one another (and rightly so!). You risk appearing callous if you say, "I'm wondering if you read my story yet because another journal already told me they want it, but I like yours better. So could you please hurry and read mine next?"

Doing this could mark you as the kind of writer who has no problem wasting other people's time. When you have strong preferences about specific journals, submit to those journals first—before you find yourself in this situation.

How Long Should I Wait Before Following Up With A Literary Journal?

This is a subjective question. But you can check out the literary magazine's website and learn the average response time, which many journals do post. If the average response time has passed and you haven't heard back, then you should be in the clear to follow up. If you're still within the response time window, keep waiting (again, unless you have good reason).

What's The Best Way To Follow Up?

Two words: Don't call. The best way to follow up is by email. If you have submitted to a lit mag using a submission manager, you can log in and take a look at the status of your material. If the editors haven't taken a look yet, you may want to go on the website and find an email address.

What Should I Say In My Follow-Up Email To A Literary Journal?

Try something like this:

Dear Editor:

On Date of Last Year I submitted my essay "Over the Moon" for your consideration. I know from your website that your average response time is three months, so I wanted to follow up to see if you've had time to consider my work yet as I haven't heard a reply. Thanks so much for your consideration.

Be Prepared To Wait...And Wait...And Wait

If you're feeling antsy waiting for responses, don't worry—it's normal. To alleviate the feeling that nothing is happening, focus on your writing instead of on the waiting game. However, if you feel you've legitimately waited long enough, then do follow up. You're absolutely entitled to!

6 Ways To Stay Calm While Waiting For Journals To Respond

Feeling anxious, distracted, and worried while editors are considering the submissions you just sent out? Are you fighting the urge to send follow-up emails—even though it hasn't been very long since you made your submissions? Are you driving yourself nuts?

Here Are 6 Things You Can To Do Stay Calm While You're Waiting For Submission Reponses

Focus on your victories. If you're feeling anxious about your submissions, you can pat yourself on the back. Why? Because if you're worrying about submissions, it means you actually sent out some submissions! Getting your work into the world is the best thing you can do for your writing career (apart from actually writing). Kudos to you for doing it!

Shift your focus to what you can control. When you're submitting for publication, the only thing you really have control over is the quality and quantity of your submissions. You can't control when a submission is read, what the reader's reaction to it will be, or whether or not you get a dreaded rejection letter. So focus on elements that are not out of your hands.

Be sure you have a submission tracking system that gives you a sense of control, so that you know who you're waiting to hear from and who has already sent a response. Then, make more submissions. Sit down to write. Enjoy taking care of the things you can control, and be confident that you're doing a good job.

Distract yourself. When you feel like your future is in someone else's hands, it's best to take your mind off your concerns. For some people, having a good, long writing session or sending a few new submissions out will be enough of a distraction. For others, a long walk, dinner with friends, or a favorite movie are great for shifting focus. When you find yourself worrying and obsessing, turn your attention in another direction—toward something good.

Change your mind about rejection letters. We remind our clients, "Each rejection gets me closer to publication." Rejection letters are good. Truly. If you're getting them, it means you're trying. And you only succeed by trying. So rejoice in rejection!

Detach from the outcome. This is a hard tactic. But if you can learn to do it, you will be well rewarded for the rest of your writing career. While you focus on what you can control, let go of what you can't. In other words, if you can't control it, don't think about it. Don't fret or agonize. Focus on the moment and let the "what ifs" go.

How does one do this difficult thing? Some people turn to religious or spiritual schools of thought. Some are more secular-minded and can shrug off the outcome of their submissions simply by thinking it through. Worrying, wondering, and fretting about your submissions while you're waiting to hear back simply will not change the outcome in any way. So why do it? Just move on.

Cultivate a positive attitude in general. If you try to stay positive and optimistic about your life, you're off to a good start! By trying to stay positive in all of your efforts, you'll find it's easier to keep your thoughts from getting away from you when you're waiting for responses from your submissions.

Learning to be patient, calm, and relaxed while you're waiting for responses to your submissions will go a long way toward an overall positive attitude in your life as a writer.

How To Withdraw A Piece From A Literary Journal

There comes a time in every writer's life when for one reason or another, you'll want to withdraw (or take back) a submission that you sent to a literary journal while it is still being considered for publication.

Here are a few of the common reasons why a writer might make a withdrawal of a submission:

- You've revised and want to resubmit a better version of the same piece.

- You've decided you don't want to see that intimate confessional poem published after all.

- You've accepted an offer from another literary journal, and the piece is no longer available.

Best-Case Scenario For Withdrawing A Poem, Story, Or Essay: Use A Submission Manager

We love online submission managers. They give a writer more control over the submission process and make everyone's lives easier.

If you have submitted your writing using an online submission manager, withdrawing a piece is easy. Simply log on, click to the piece in question, then make your withdrawal.

NOTE: If you have submitted a group of poems using a submission manager, you may need to withdraw the ENTIRE group, then resubmit that group minus the one or two poems that you are withdrawing.

Making Your Withdrawal Request By Email

A much less reliable way to withdraw a submission is to find an email address and send an email requesting that your piece be removed from consideration.

You may want to note in your subject line: *Withdrawal request for Name of Piece, by Writer Name.*

You don't need to give an explanation of your reasons for the withdrawal. Keep your note short:

Dear Editor:

If you have not already read my essay "Over the Moon," I would like to request that it be withdrawn from consideration. If possible, please reply and let me know you received this note. Thank you so much. I appreciate your time.

You may or may not receive a response. We don't recommend sending multiple follow-ups. Sometimes, editors do get emails but simply don't reply.

Making A Request For Withdrawal By Mail

Generally, we don't recommend using mail to make a request to withdraw your work. The postal service takes too long; email ensures that your note will arrive in editors' hands quickly.

If you must make your request by mail, just be polite, brief, and professional.

What If Your Withdrawal Request Is Accidentally Ignored?

Literary journals get a lot of email, mail, faxes, etc. Correspondence gets lost or shuffled. Frankly, it happens with some regularity that a writer's request for withdrawal is lost. Suddenly, a writer who asked for his or her piece to be removed from consideration finds an offer of publication in the mail.

If this happens to you, and the piece is not available for any reason, don't panic. You did your part. Sometimes, email requests for withdrawals do get misplaced—but if you've got a copy of your sent request, any misunderstandings that arise due to disorganization at a given literary journal won't be your fault.

In a best-case scenario, the editor will be so head-over-heels in love with your work that he or she won't mind considering an alternate manuscript. Try offering a substitute for the withdrawn piece. Or, if the piece has already been published, try offering reprint rights to publish it (you can't offer "first rights" if it has already appeared or is slated to appear somewhere else).

How And When To Reject An Acceptance

Aside from researching literary markets and writing cover/query letters, part of our job at Writer's Relief is advising clients on their paths to publication. And though we most often write about helping writers submit work in order to achieve a coveted acceptance letter, we also help our clients maneuver the complicated territory of turning down acceptances.

Why Would A Writer Consider Turning Down An Acceptance?

In a perfect world, writers would thoroughly research every single magazine to which they submit—including reading sample publications cover to cover. However, this is not always feasible for writers for obvious reasons. Typically, writers will do some cursory research and then send their work out for consideration. Then, inevitably, the rejection letters start rolling in.

Trouble occurs when an author receives an acceptance letter from a literary journal that seemed like a great fit at first glance—but then, the author begins to second-guess. *What if a bigger journal wants my work, and I simply haven't heard back from them yet?*

How To Decide Whether Or Not To Accept An Acceptance:

1. Take a deep breath. Getting emotionally worked up will only make things worse. Before you panic over having to give up your dreams at seeing your piece appear in your favorite top-tier publication, or before you hyperventilate over the thought of having an uncomfortable conversation with the editor of the accepting journal, just breathe. And then (calmly) move along to step 2.

2. Do some research. It might not seem like this is the "right" home for your work at first, but if you take the time to read a few issues, you might be surprised to find yourself in very good company among other talented and noteworthy writers. Maybe the publication is right for you and your piece and you just weren't familiar enough with it to realize. And you might be surprised by how much you genuinely like this publication— maybe you would rather have your piece guaranteed to appear in this one rather than in the one you were initially holding out for (that you haven't heard back from yet).

3. Broaden your horizons. If you're slightly disappointed with your acceptance because it's from one of the "smaller" publications that you submitted to, take a step back. There are actually many advantages to having smaller journals in your list of credits. Small and mid-range journals tend to be advocates for new and emerging writers, and many of them nominate for impressive writing awards such as the Pushcart Prize. The likelihood of a big-shot journal accepting an author with zero publication credits and then nominating the work for a prize: not impossible, but not likely.

4. Listen to your heart. Before you can gracefully proceed, you'll need to reach a firm decision based on your true feelings. You don't want to agree to the acceptance only to feel disappointed when the issue comes out, and you don't want to regret turning down the acceptance if your holdout ends up turning the piece down. So before you even think about how you'll handle moving forward, be sure of your decision and prepare for the consequences. If you decline the acceptance, feeling sure of yourself will take the sting out of an angry editor; if you take the acceptance, being firm will ensure you're satisfied seeing your piece released in the issue.

How To Proceed Once You've Made Your Decision:

If you've decided to accept your first offer of publication, that's easy: Email the editor promptly with an appreciative message accepting the offer.

If you've decided not to take the acceptance, you'll need to send a gracious and apologetic note—especially promptly. We never advise lying; you might tell the editor that though you appreciate the acceptance from the bottom of your heart, you've decided to go a different direction.

You can leave it at that, or you can offer the editor another piece in its place—but don't expect the editor to accept the alternative piece(s). He or she might be open to it or might be miffed, and you'll need to be prepared for either reaction. If the editor is irritated, you might not be able to submit to that market ever again.

After all, editors spend a lot of time coming to their decisions on what work to publish, and you don't want to burn any bridges. But if you've been true to yourself in reaching your decision, you should be satisfied with the outcome, whatever it may be.

How To Ask An Editor To Reconsider Your Poem, Story, Or Essay

There are circumstances that may make it worth your while to resubmit a piece to a literary magazine.

For example: Say you decide to revise a piece that you submitted a while ago but did not get published. You're sure that you're a better writer now and that the piece may get some traction because of your revisions. You may want to consider resubmitting.

Or, say you want to submit a short prose piece or group of poems that you'd sent out a few years ago. You received some glowing rejection letters but no takers. Since that time, the market has become more favorable to your particular style. You wonder: Is it time to give it another try?

Often, the masthead at many literary magazines will change regularly. So the editor who rejected your work two years ago may no longer work at that magazine. Although resending a story or poem counts as a resubmission, your work will likely be given consideration with fresh eyes if some time has passed. The magazine may have decided to go a new direction or to pursue a theme that is more closely related to your work.

Also, if your story was rejected with an encouraging note (such as, "we liked your piece but do not have room for it right now"), then you may do well to resubmit in the hopes that the editor will be interested in publishing your work now that some time has passed and more space is available.

Sometimes, when editors at literary journals do NOT rotate regularly, you still may be in a good position to resubmit. However, sending the exact same work to the exact same editor may not give you the best shot at getting an acceptance letter—especially if you're resubmitting overly soon.

If your work has been roundly rejected, then revise it! Go the extra mile, dig deep, and make your work truly better. That way, you'll have the best shot at getting an acceptance for your resubmission.

If An Editor Invites You To Resubmit Or Requests (Or Suggests) Changes

If you get feedback from an editor, we recommend you proceed with caution. If you like your original work as is but are willing to tweak it based on a single editor's feedback, then you can make the suggested mod-ifications and send your work off to the editor who requested them.

But we don't recommend that you start resubmitting your work every time you make a change. That would drive editors crazy and would no doubt earn you a bad reputation in the close-knit writing community.

Keep in mind that one editor may ask you to add a particular paragraph, while another editor might ask you to delete it. Listen to the voice inside you—the voice that told you to write your work in a specific way to begin with—and make your changes with caution and respect for your own creative ideas!

Cautions About Resubmitting Poems, Stories, and Essays

Because more and more literary journals—both print magazines and online literary journals—are beginning to use online submission management systems, the way to resubmit is changing.

Submission managers are tracking what you submit, when you submitted it, what comments editors had about your work (why it was accepted or rejected), and more.

As a result, editors will be able to track whether they've already considered a piece that you're resubmitting. For this reason, you may want to detail the precise reason for your resubmission in the comments section of the submission manager. Make a gentle (not flashy) argument for being reconsidered. Then, keep your fingers crossed!

But Can't I Just Change The Title And They'll Never Know?

We don't recommend changing the title of your work to hide the fact that it is a resubmission. If you've revised the work significantly and those revisions merit a new title, then that's probably acceptable because it is an authentic and necessary change. Editors will not appreciate sneakiness, however, and you wouldn't want to become blacklisted within the writing community! Honesty is the best policy.

Also, keep in mind that you do not want to resubmit your work too often. Resubmitting a piece to the same markets is not a good strategy for getting published. As writers, we've got to be continually pushing ourselves. We must search for new stories, new combinations of words, new ideas.

It's always better to submit new work whenever you can. However, resubmitting under certain circumstances can sometimes yield positive results.

When you're considering making a resubmission, use your best judgment. Each writer's position is unique. What we've offered you are broad guidelines based on our experience. Just be sure you're polite, professional, and thoughtful about your manner of resubmission.

Part Four

Special Considerations For Poetry

Submission Strategies And Pointers Just For Poets

How To Group Your Poems When Submitting For Publication

If you're wondering how to choose the right poems to submit to a literary journal, how many to include, and how to increase your chances of publication, read on!

But as always, be sure to follow an individual literary journal's guidelines when submitting your poems to an editor. The tips we offer are suggestions, not rules.

How Many Poems Should I Include In A Single Submission?

Generally, literary journals ask their writers to submit between three and five poems in one submission. Few journals will accept more than ten pages of poetry in one submission. That said, the number of poems can vary, so read the guidelines.

Can I Submit Just One Poem At A Time?

If you have very strong reasons for feeling that your one poem would be a perfect fit at a journal but none of your other poems would be, you might want to explain that in your cover letter.

An editor may be willing to consider your solitary poem if you give him or her a good reason.

Should I Group Related Poems? Or Poems That Stand Alone?

There are no best practices in terms of whether to submit poems that stand alone or poems that are thematically related. But there are pros and cons.

Submitting Related Poems – The Pros

- If an editor likes your voice, he or she may choose to print all of the poems because they're related.
- Long poems that are broken down into many parts can be very compelling. They can demonstrate a big vision.
- If the poems are about a specific topic, you can submit the group to a journal that focuses on theme.

Submitting Related Poems – The Cons

- If an editor chooses only one poem of your related poems, he or she might "break" the flow of the complete series and also leave the other poems orphaned if they can't stand alone.
- If an editor doesn't like your voice or theme, then you won't be getting any poems accepted...because all the poems are related and possibly sound the same.

Submitting Stand-Alone Poems – The Pros

- Show off your diversity. If an editor doesn't like one poem, you still have a chance because the other poems are different.
- With five unrelated poems you might have a better shot at seeing at least one of them published than with five related poems that can't be separated.

Submitting Stand-Alone Poems – The Cons

- If an editor really loves one of your poems for its unique qualities, there's less of a chance he or she will also want the others, which will be quite different.
- You may need to research a greater number of markets in order to the find the right journals for all of your individual poems.
- You'll have limited ability to submit to theme issues, since only some poems will be appropriate for submission.
- Even if you're not grouping by theme, you probably wouldn't want your kid-friendly rhyme mixed in with your edgy adult free verse.

Sometimes It's Best Not To Overthink Poem Groupings

If your instincts are tugging you to create a certain group of poems, there may be a reason for it. There are no rules about how best to group poems for submission. It's all about your creativity and your intuition.

Length Matters: Poetry

When submitting to lit mags, poets should consider limiting their poems to one page—two pages at the most—*when possible.*

Here's why this strategy tends to get results: Given the limited amount of space they have available, editors forced to choose between two equally good submissions will often choose the one that's shorter. Editors want to showcase as many writers as they can per issue. And do not assume that the editor will take the time to trim your submission if it's too long.

Certainly, there are some journals and magazines that will accept longer works, but by submitting shorter pieces, you will be able to approach a greater number of publications. And the more places you can submit your work, the more likely you'll be able to earn a publication credit.

5 Tips For Trimming Your Poems

Some poets talk about an economy of language in poetry. Whatever you call it, it means getting rid of absolutely all unnecessary words and phrases that don't carry their weight and then some.

Poetic Liposuction: 5 Ways To Trim The Fat From Your Poems

Nix unnecessary adjectives. Do you really need the words "loamy and earthy" to describe "soil"? Doesn't "loamy," in context, already imply "earthy"? And for that matter, isn't all soil "earth"? If one adjective can do the job of two, cut one out and rejoice. A good poet doesn't ramble; she or he writes just enough—and not a word more.

Turn adverbs into regular verbs. Rather than "he walked briskly and with purpose" or "she sank dejectedly downward in her chair, try "he strode" or "she slumped in her chair." Of course, this goes for prose writers too!

Don't write the way you talk. In everyday speech, we can be lazy. We can beat around the bush, gossip, digress, and make lots of small talk. We've got time to make our point.

But in poetry, brevity wins. Instead of "I wanted to ask him to ask me to dance," use fewer words: "Would he ask me to dance?" Again, prose writers take note.

Stop thinking like a prose writer. If you're writing a poem, you're not writing a short story.

Get to the essence of your poem. Dig into the core, find the beating heart, and cut it out of the body of your poem (gross, but stay with us). The heart of your poem will probably keep beating, even without all the extra verbiage of the body. And if it doesn't, that's what drafts are for. You can always go back to the original version.

You may need to take classes or attend writing conferences to learn how to be more concise in your writing.

The Bottom Line For Editing Poems

Don't let the fear of writing too many words hold you back during your first draft. Always follow your inspiration.

But remember: Cut fearlessly. Be bold. How much can you say in as few words as possible? The worst that will happen is you'll need to revert to a saved draft.

5 Poetry Turnoffs That Make Editors Cringe

Some poetic angles/strategies seem not to work with many editors. Here are some of the trickier elements that can (sometimes) be turnoffs for editors.

Long poems and difficult spacing. As previously stated, poems that are one page long tend to be more readily accepted than any other length poem. Also, watch your margins. A poem that is too many characters wide may not fit on the narrow pages of print literary magazines or the page layout of an online journal's website. Tightly constructed poems are easier to publish and more readily accepted.

Clichés. Nature, love, and death are said to be the big three topics for writers. So if you're going to address any of these subjects, make sure that you're approaching them in a truly new way. Tip: The only way you can be sure your writing is not cliché is by reading poetry. Lots of poetry. If you love poetry, read and support the magazines that keep poetry alive.

One-word titles. Titles like "Death" or "Friendship" tend to be more often overlooked by editors. Consider the wording of your title just as important as the rest of your poem.

Double-spacing. Some poems call for double-spacing. But based on what we hear from lit mag editors, most poems don't need it. New writers tend to fall back on double-spaced lines to make their poems look more impressive—but editors aren't fooled. Use double-spacing only if you have a good reason.

Centered lines. There is an inclination among some newer poets to center the text of poems. However, this is considered amateurish, and editors have been known to be dismissive of centered poems.

However, if there is a reason other than "it looks nice" that your poem must be centered, then by all means, stick to your guns. Hopefully, you'll connect with an editor who enjoys your work and will not dismiss your poem simply because of the center justification.

One Final Note About Poetry Format

The above tips are based on the experiences of Writer's Relief in helping poets publish their poems. However, we do not advocate writing poetry only for the market. If the muse moves you to write a certain way, you should do what makes you happy. Writing poetry is a very personal matter, and the decisions you make about your poems should be made with care and authority—regardless of the market.

The most important thing is your attitude: You're studying poetry, reading poetry, and knowing who you are and what you're about.

As always, be sure that when you submit, you've researched the proper markets, proofread your work, and followed all appropriate guidelines.

How To Publish A Book Of Poems

If you've written so many poems that you're considering publishing a poetry collection, there are a number of ways you can accomplish your goal. But before we tell you how, there are a few things you should keep in mind.

First, poets approach Writer's Relief every day asking us how we can help them make money on their poetry. As you know, there isn't much profit in publishing individual poems in lit mags. The same holds true for poetry books.

Traditional, big publishing houses typically do not publish the work of unknown or moderately known poets because there simply isn't a large audience. And because there's no money in poetry, literary agents tend not to represent poets (with the exception of the very famous). So that's the bad news.

But the good news is that poetry readers and writers have created a strong alternative market to big New York publishing houses. If you've got time, talent, and luck, you may be able to get your book of poems published and maybe even make some money. It's best to have a solid list of publication credits for your individual poems before you start asking people to publish your poems en masse. If your bio is strong and testifies to your skill, here are some ways to publish a chapbook or collection of poems.

How To Publish A Book Of Poems

Enter chapbook contests. If you've amassed a collection of poems that might not be long enough for a full poetry book, you might try entering a chapbook contest. Although the rules vary, chapbook contests generally want between 25 and 60 pages of poetry. Most chapbook contests are sponsored by universities or small presses. There may be an entry fee, but there is usually a payout for the winner in the form of publication—and sometimes even a monetary prize. If your poems are very strong, entering chapbook contests might be a good way to get your poetry chapbook or collection published.

Approach small presses. If your collection of poetry is too big for a chapbook, consider approaching small presses (independent publishers) with your poems. To do this, you'll need to have strong publishing credentials. Again, universities and small presses are the heart of contemporary poetry, so do the proper research and send your queries their way.

Self-publish. Keep in mind that self-publishing requires that you do all the legwork regarding distribution. Your book will not appear on bookshelves unless you do something to get it there. If you'd like a way to easily share your poetry with your family and friends, self-publishing may be a good option. But if you're taking the self-publishing route because you think it's an easier way to reach a large audience, think again. Unless you're prepared to do lots of promotion and marketing, your book will not reach far and wide.

Even though there isn't a strong mainstream market for poetry, the independent markets are thriving. So keep your chin high and your pen flying, and you just might see your poetry book in print.

Part Five

Special Considerations For Stories And Personal Essays

Submission Strategies And Pointers
Just For Short Prose Writers

Length Matters: Keeping Short Prose Short

Many editors of literary journals, especially online literary journals, are favoring shorter short stories than what used to be the norm (about 5,000 words). These days, that word count is around 3,500. The same holds true for short personal essays (creative nonfiction).

Word count matters to editors. If you want to slim down your short prose, we've got some word-fat busting exercises for you! Soon you'll be showing off your trim short shorts all summer (and winter) long!

How To Shorten Your Short Prose

1. First, change your mind. There's a belief among some writers that a lot of meaning needs a LOT of words. But that's just not true. BIG short stories can come in little packages!

A short story or essay can pack just as much meaning and experience into the text as a long story that sprawls. Concise and focused writing often leads to a bigger emotional impact. Stories with action that starts on page one tend to get more attention than those that fight for momentum.

Is it easy to write "short"? Nope. But that's why editors (in general) favor shorter shorts. Writers who go the extra mile to trim, tighten, and edit tend to earn editors' favor.

So don't be afraid to tighten things up!

2. Start on the right foot. In a best-case scenario, your short story develops before you put pen to paper (or fingers to keyboard). How you envision the beginning of your short prose piece can impact how it turns out.

For example: If you imagine a short story that's going to follow the life of a salesman from his third grade play to his three marriages to his death, you're going to have a really, really long short story. In fact, you might have a novella.

But if you envision a short story that's a snippet of that man's life—maybe a meaningful dinner party or the birth of a child—frankly, your story will do a better job of delving into the meaning for the moment than if you bite off more than your short story can chew.

3. Use your tight focus lens. Imagine your short prose is a camera. To make the most of a short work, focus tightly on one character or one moment. Explore the moment from every angle. Sometimes, very small moments can have huge, unthinkably consequential meanings. The moment can be mundane (a man picks up his daughter whom he sees every other weekend) to the exceptional (a woman sits in the waiting room of the ER). Either way, there's a lot of gravity to discover in the "small" moments.

4. Consider a character sketch. A short story or essay doesn't have to "do" much; it can just "be." A short story or essay is not necessarily like a novel or a memoir, which often has a particular kind of momentum that builds from one scene to the next. For this reason, a short story is a great place to work up a character sketch. Explore a character's strengths and flaws. Perhaps there's a quiet moment at the end of the story in which the character has the opportunity to change (this would be a climactic moment). Whether or not he or she decides to make that change will give your character sketch some shape.

5. Revisit your existing short prose. Sometimes it's possible to find a shorter story within a longer one. For example, you might revisit an old short story or essay, identify a key moment, and then write a new short piece that focuses specifically on that moment (rather than offering a series of scenes leading to that moment). Or you might consider doing a character sketch based on a character you already know from a previous short work—you might even learn something new!

Short Prose: Defining And Mixing Genres

The genres of short prose writing can be very confusing. For example, some writers will call their personal essay a story, and others will call their essay a memoir. To make matters even more complicated, a number of literary magazines are beginning to accept what is commonly called mixed genre writing. It's important to understand the difference between the types of short prose, whether you're writing a personal essay, short story, memoir, commentary, or mixed genre piece.

What Is A Short Story?

A short story is a work of fictional prose. Its characters may be loosely based on real people, and its plot may be inspired by an actual event; but overall more of the story is made up than real. Or the story can be entirely fiction. Short stories may be literary, or they may conform to genre standards (i.e., a romance short story, a science-fiction short story, a horror story, etc.).

Short Story Example #1: A writer is inspired by a car explosion in his town. He writes a story based on the real explosion and set in a similar town, but showing the made-up experiences of his characters (who may be partly based on real life).

Short Story Example #2: An author writes a story based on a made-up explosion, set in a made-up town, and showing the made-up experiences of his fictional characters.

What Is A Personal Or Narrative Essay (Creative Nonfiction)? What Is An Academic Essay? What's The Difference?

Though factual, the personal essay (sometimes called a narrative essay) can feel like a short story, complete with characters and a plot arc. A personal essay is a short work of nonfiction that is not academic (that is, not a dissertation or scholarly exploration or criticism, etc.).

In a personal essay, the writer recounts his or her personal experiences or opinions. In an academic essay, the writer's personal involvement with the subject does not play a large part in the narrative (or plot line).

Sometimes the purpose of a personal essay is simply to entertain. Some personal essays may have a meditative or even dogmatic feel; a personal essay may illustrate a writer's experiences in order to make an argument for the writer's opinion. Some personal essays may cite other texts (like books, stories, or poems), but the focus of the citation is not to make an academic point. Rather, emphasis is on the writer's emotional journey and insight.

Personal Essay Example: A writer pens the story of his experience at the scene of a car explosion in his town. The work is short enough for publication in a literary journal and focuses on the author's perspective.

What Is A Commentary?

The personal essay form and commentary may sometimes overlap, but it may be helpful to make some distinctions. A commentary is often very short (a few hundred words) and more journalistic in tone than a personal essay. It fits nicely as a column in a newspaper or on a personal blog. The writing can be more newsy than literary.

Some very short nonfiction pieces may be better suited to newspapers than to literary journals; however, literary magazines have been known to publish commentary-type pieces that have a literary bent.

Commentary Example: A writer tells the story of a car explosion in his town to illustrate the point that the police are not vigilant enough about people throwing flaming marshmallows out their windows.

What Is A Memoir?

Memoir generally refers to book-length works of nonfiction about the author's life, written from the author's perspective. Memoir does not generally refer to short personal essays. If you're writing a short piece based on your real-life experiences, editors of literary journals will identify this as a personal essay. If you're writing a book about an experience, it's a memoir. A collection of interrelated personal essays may constitute a memoir.

Memoir Example: A writer composes a full-length book about his experiences after a car explosion in his town.

What Is A Nonfiction Short Story?

There's no such thing as a nonfiction short story. Short stories are inherently fiction (with or without real-life inspiration). Personal essays are not fictional.

Example: None.

So What Is Mixed Genre Writing?

Mixed genre writing is creative work that does not fit in any of the previously mentioned genres. Mixed genre writing blends some elements of fiction with elements of nonfiction in a very deliberate way.

Mixed Genre Example #1: A professional accountant named John Jones is writing a story about a man named John Jones, who is John Jones and lives John Jones' life—except that the fictional John Jones one day decides to leave his real-life accounting job, and live his dream of being a rock star.

Mixed Genre Example #2: A writer decides to compose a family history, using pictures and documents from her family albums. But sometimes her story veers into fiction. She finds herself embellishing elements or omitting characters. The result is a story that's better than the one she might tell if she simply stayed with the facts.

NOTE: Sometimes the term "mixed genre" is defined in terms of the novel or book. A mixed genre novel might be a novel that mixes science-fiction elements with characteristics of a legal thriller. Or a mixed genre novel might play fast and loose with fact and fiction. If you're going to refer to your book as mixed genre, be clear about what you mean.

Tips On Writing Mixed Genre

If you're going to write mixed genre prose, do so with care. Mixed genre writing often has a kind of self-aware, almost tongue-in-cheek, element to it—a wink to the reader who is not fooled by the mixing of fiction and nonfiction, even if the lines are blurry. Mixed genre can be considered experimental, so it's important that the writing be exceptionally smart in order to live up to the demands of the (mixed) genre.

Short Story Or Novella?

How do you know if your short prose is a short story or a novella? How long is a short story? A novella? What's the difference? If you want to get your short story or novella published, you'll need to know who is publishing your type of fiction—and you'll need to know the best way to target your writing to literary agents and editors of literary magazines.

How Long Is A Novella?

A novella is a "short book." As such, a novella is considerably longer than a short story but shorter than a novel. A novella must be able to stand on its own as a book, but the exact word count is not set in stone: 30,000 to 60,000 words may be an appropriate length for a novella in most markets.

Who Is Publishing Novellas?

Imagine the weight and size of a typical novel (80,000 to 100,000 words) when you hold it in your hand. Now imagine holding a slim, 30,000-word book—almost a pamphlet—in your hand. In order for a publisher to justify the production and marketing overhead of taking on a novella, the publisher must give the reader a valuable experience that justifies the price of the book.

The trouble is, the profit margin of a novella can be lower than the profit margin of a novel in certain circumstances. For that reason, few big publishers will take on a stand-alone novella—except in certain circumstances. When a novella is published, it is often bound in a collection of novellas by various authors or the same author, creating an anthology.

Because novellas are difficult to market as print novels, they have become very popular in the world of digital publishing. E-publishers are readily taking on novellas of all genres, and readers of e-books are on the rise. In fact, some e-publishers prefer novellas to novels because some readers of electronic formats prefer shorter books—and a good novella can pack a lot of story into a limited number of pages!

How Long Is A Short Story?

Although a short story could be as long as 30,000 words, stories of that length begin to become too bulky for their genre. Generally speaking, editors of literary magazines are readily publishing short stories of approximately 3,500 words or less. Some publish longer stories, but our clients have the most markets available to them when they submit stories that are less than 3,500 words.

Short stories published in online literary magazines are often held to even smaller word counts, sometimes as little as 1,000 words or less. Flash fiction can be even shorter. The Internet has dramatically changed the way modern readers approach fiction and prose. The current trend is that shorter short stories are more readily published than longer ones.

However, the longer short story isn't dead. It's just a matter of seeking out the markets that are open to higher word counts. Some online journals are publishing longer stories (especially given that print costs don't apply when a long story is accepted).

Make Your Short Prose Stand Out In A Crowd

Imagine for a moment that you're the editor of a well-known literary journal. Every day, hundreds of short stories cross your desk in a relentless stream, blurring together, melting into one huge pile of "no." For the most part, none of the short story submissions stand out in a crowd.

And then—BAM! A story strikes a chord deep within you. Now that's something you might want to publish. It goes in the other pile, the much smaller and elusive batch of wonderful "yes."

But floating to the top of that river of submissions takes effort, persistence, and a few tricks up your sleeve. Here are ways to make your story stand out:

1. Open your short prose piece with a bang. Unless he's turned into a giant cockroach overnight, starting your story with your main character waking up is as average as it gets. You have a small space in which to tell your story, so get straight to the point—try dropping the audience in medias res (right into the heart of the action), and get them excited for the ride. NOTE: You don't need to be flashy to be impressive: a moment of quiet intensity and meaning can work as well as an exploding car.

2. Keep it short. Pack a punch in very few words. Throw away unnecessary frills.

3. Focus on larger-than-life characters. Dull characters make for dull short stories. While you want your characters to be relatable, you don't want them to be boring. If they are dynamic, have their own unique voices, and approach their world in distinctive ways, they'll stick in a reader's mind...and so will your story.

4. Paint your world vividly. Whether it's a bustling metropolis or the middle of the unforgiving Sahara, the setting in which your story takes place influences everything that happens within it. Don't just plop your characters into a generic town—create a specific environment and reveal to the audience the intricacies therein.

5. Keep the stakes high. There's a certain aspect of human nature that likes to experience intense situations vicariously. So never let the lifeline of your story run flat. Every decision your characters make should propel the story forward, keeping the plot taut and engaging. The higher the stakes, the bigger the catharsis your readers will experience when the conflict is resolved.

Publish A Collection Of Short Stories Or Essays

We're approached by countless writers every year who want help submitting their short story or essay collections to literary agents. Is it possible to get a collection of short prose published? Yes. But it's not easy.

Major publishers want novels, memoirs, or narrative nonfiction books because they sell. On rare occasion, they will consider novellas or collections of short stories. Short prose collections are harder to place because editors are often reluctant to take chances on unknown writers.

Before you protest about the number of successful anthologies on the market, be aware that anthologies are generally collections of stories by a number of different authors—collections appealing to those who are looking for a particular theme or subject matter. Anthologies of work by a single, relatively unknown author tend to be difficult to sell.

Here are some things you can do to improve your odds of finding a publisher for your collection of short stories or essays.

Publish selected works. It's easier to sell a collection if you've had at least a few short pieces previously published in reputable literary journals. Submit individual stories to quality magazines on a regular basis, and with each publication credit, your credibility will increase.

Theme. It helps if the stories have a common theme or subject to tie your short works together.

Go for a book. Some agents recommend scrapping the whole idea of a collection and refashioning it into a novel—or even a "novel-in-stories" or "memoir in episodes." They might also recommend selling the collection as part of a two-book deal, with the collection designed to generate interest in the second book.

Enter as many writing competitions as possible. An award-winning story or essay can land a publishing deal. It can also boost a writer's self-confidence—always a bonus.

Consider small presses. There are far more small presses than big publishing houses, and they often specialize in niche marketing. They also tend to publish out of love for the genre, and may be more receptive to a collection if they are impressed by the quality of your work.

Get a literary agent. If you have an agent, your chances of selling a collection are better than for unagented writers. To get an agent for a short prose collection, you'll need a strong bio.

Get schooled. Collections are sometimes easier to sell when their authors have top-notch credentials, which can include graduating from a quality MFA program. Is a degree necessary? No. But sometimes it helps.

Your author platform. With creative nonfiction, you're selling your personality and your experiences. If you have any notoriety, you'll find it easier to publish your essay collection. But if not, don't worry! It's the strength of your story that counts most.

BONUS!

How To Be "The Complete Package" As A Writer

Take A Look At The Big Picture
Of Your Writing Career

The 7 Signs Of A Healthy Submission Strategy

How Many Of These Seven Signs Of Success Are Showing Up In Your Writing Life?

Your work is strong. You read regularly and you put energy and effort into your craft. You've spent your time in workshops, lectures, and seminars at writing conferences. You've become really good at accepting both praise and criticism. You're beginning to have a sense of confidence in your writing. And it's starting to show.

You know the drill. Along with mastering your craft, you've learned the publishing industry etiquette that covers how to submit to literary journals. You know the proper format for a manuscript. You know the importance of professional proofreading. You know what your cover letter should say. Your submission packets and electronic submissions are polished, professional, and attractive.

You're submitting regularly (and writing regularly). You take your submissions as seriously as you take your writing, and that means you're setting aside time for both at regular intervals. By consistently sending out submissions, you have a better chance of getting more publication offers.

You look at rejection letters positively. You no longer feel a debilitating pang of disappointment when your work is turned down. You look at your rejection letters as badges of honor: They mean you're not letting the world get you down. Your work is out there; you're trying; you're a positive thinker.

You're not afraid of numbers. Along with being positive about your rejection letters, you've also made it past a writer's urge to "just quit" after a few submissions. You understand that submissions are, to some extent, a numbers game. You know that if a work is reasonably strong, there is definitely somebody out there who wants to read it. So you're persistent. You'll keep sending your work out for as long as it takes until it finds a good home.

You're getting better at knowing where *not* to send your work. In the beginning, you sent your writing to any random journal. Now, you're being more selective. You're spending more time searching through market books and researching online for lit mag. (Or you're working with Writer's Relief, so you know the research is spot-on.)

You're always after something better. Your writing is getting better. Your submissions are getting better. Each day, you're pushing yourself to be the best you can be. And each time you think you've made it to the top, you discover an exciting new peak to climb.

Does This Sound Like You?

If so, congratulations! You've got a healthy submission strategy and the mindset to go the distance.

But if you're feeling frustrated, pessimistic, or just too busy to carve out the time needed to develop a strong submission strategy, it may be time to contact Writer's Relief. Our submission strategists are more than trained motivators who are there to keep you writing; they're also experienced professionals who will regularly and expertly guide your submissions into just the right hands.

If You Are Going To Hire A Submission Service...

Since we've mentioned our own services, we also want to give you some pointers in case you decide to approach ANY submission service for help with your submissions to literary journals. We hope this helps.

There are resources and companies available to you, but some are better than others. When deciding how to submit your work to literary journals or to agents, it's important to have a solid grasp of two key factors:

1. Know the publishing protocol. Before you trust anyone else to make your submissions for you, it's a good idea to know how the industry works. This way, you'll be more likely to pick up on anything that doesn't seem like a good practice (for example, sending an agent more than one book proposal at once is generally a no-no).

2. Know your goals. Most writers have the same basic goals: to be published and share their writing with others. But it's important to keep your goals realistic. Start with mid-tier, reputable journals, and work your way up. Don't expect to be published in *The New Yorker* or the *Paris Review* in your first submission round. And be wary of any company that promises pie-in-the-sky results.

How To Find The Best Submission Help

Every writer is unique, and that means every writer has unique needs. When deciding if you want outside help in developing a submission strategy, ask yourself the following questions:

How much help with submissions do you want? Some writers just want a list of markets that will review their work; they'll do the rest. Other writers want all-inclusive attention, so that they don't have to worry about any part of their submission strategy. Choosing a full service option will allow you to spend all your time writing.

Write down your wish list for getting help with your submissions. What do you want someone else to do for you? Write your cover letter? Track editors' responses to your poems? Etc.

Do you need a support system? It's important to have a reliable, tried-and-true support system of people you trust who are highly educated about the publishing industry and can advise you when questions arise.

If you're going to use a submission assistance company, confirm that you'll have a knowledgeable professional on your team to help you overcome the inevitable bumps on the road to publishing.

What will you "pay" to reach your goals? No submission service is free (not even if you do it yourself). If you want someone to prepare your submissions or simply to provide targeted research, then you'll need to have a budget that covers the many hours a company will need to spend on these tasks.

If you go it alone, you'll have to "pay yourself" with your time spent researching (which means you'll not only have to find markets that work for you, you'll also need to eliminate thousands that don't).

Weigh Your Options

Here are a few of the options available to you if you're considering third-party assistance when making submissions.

Hire a submission service. If you're going to hire a company like Writer's Relief to help you, ask questions. Be sure you understand what you're getting into. And be wary of promises to make all your dreams come true or requirements involving contracts that lock you in. Here are a few sample questions to ask:

- How do you research markets? Is the research personalized?
- How many clients do you have? Any credible writers?
- What are your rates? Do you take commission?
- Who will be my contact at the company?
- Is any writer accepted or are there standards? What genres do you work with?
- Can I quit whenever I want?
- Are you acquiring any rights to my work?

Hire a personal assistant. We consider ourselves a team of personal assistants who have specialized knowledge about the publishing industry and work offsite (not in our clients' homes). You can hire a personal secretary to help you, but make sure it is someone with publishing experience.

Otherwise, you could waste as much time teaching someone to make your submissions as it would take for you to do them yourself. Also, keep in mind that expertise matters when tough questions arise, and you may need to turn to professionals for answers.

DIY database websites and market books. If you're reading this book, you might have the right kind of self-starting attitude to conduct your own successful submission strategy. Remember: You don't need anyone's help making submissions if you've got the focus, education, time, and drive to get it done.

Resources On The Writer's Relief Website

Interested in more information about how to improve your writing career? Here are just a few of the many resources on the Writer's Relief website!

Submit Write Now! Our weekly e-publication features interviews, news, strategies, tips, publishing leads, contests, and so much more!

Writers Classifieds Pages. Find up-to-the-minute lists of publishing leads, contests, calls for submissions, anthologies, writing conferences, etc.

Publishing Tool Kit. Our tool kit answers just about every question you might have about how to develop a successful submission strategy. Get your tool kit today! Some of the topics include:

- How To Get Published: A Step-By-Step Guide For Beginning And Intermediate Writers
- Grammar And Usage
- Short Story Submissions: How To Submit Short Stories For Publication
- Poetry Submissions: How To Submit Your Poetry For Publication
- Web Design: Online Marketing And Promotion Strategies For Writers
- How To Handle Rejection: A Writer's Secret Weapon Against Rejection
- Writers Associations: Local And National Organizations For Writers

Video Tutorials. Step-by-step guides for people who aren't sure how to make submissions using email or online submission managers.

Free consultation with a submission strategist. See if Writer's Relief has a plan that will work for your submissions to agents or literary magazines.

How An Author Website Enhances Your Writing Career

As more and more information moves online, Googleability is becoming increasingly important for writer who want to build a reputation. Editors and potential fans will Google you out of curiosity. Be ready for them!

If you don't have an author website yet, it may be time to consider getting one.

With an author website, you can...

- Be in the right place at the right time...because the Web is open 24/7.
- Integrate your social networks...so friends can become fans.
- Help establish strong branding.
- Make it easier for editors to find and connect with you.
- Give readers an easy way to follow you.
- Showcase your already published short stories, essays, or poetry.
- Link in literary journals and magazines (and engage with them).
- Be linked into by online literary journals and other sites.

Here are just a few of the essential functions of a good author website:

Feature Your Writing Portfolio

Showcasing your works online is a fantastic way to hook editors and fans (just be sure you know the rules about previously published writing before you post your words online). By including links to magazines and online literary journals that published your work, you demonstrate that you're on top of your game. Your site is also the place where you can introduce other projects you're working on too!

Hint: As we've previously stated, literary agents have approached our clients because of a short story or poem published in a lit mag. Having a website makes it easy for agents—and other key industry players—to find you.

If you're promoting your author website, it's very likely that someone important could read and become intrigued by your work. But if you don't have an author website, it's more difficult for people to connect with you.

Offer Detailed Background Info

When writing your cover letter, include the address of your website. Editors will visit your site to learn more about you. A cover letter bio can only go so far. But a website has no limits! People come to your website to find out more about the real you. When you give visitors what they want, you make fans and friends!

You can share more details about yourself on your website. What inspired you to write? Who are your favorite authors? What made you decide to pursue trying to be a published writer?

Your author website can show important people that you're likable, friendly, professional, warm...all the things one hopes for in a partner. So relax, have fun, and be yourself! If your site gives off a good vibe, that energy will carry through into your other endeavors.

Build A Fan Base

When readers like what they see, they'll be more likely visit again. Agents and editors may want to keep an eye on you as an up-and-coming writer. A regularly updated website helps with that.

Demonstrate Your Relevance

By expanding your presence online, you show that you understand how today's world works. It's a digital age, and most writers who are hoping to make a name for themselves do have websites.

If possible, try to work with a website design company that understands the specific needs of creative writers (including budgeting and ease of use!). To get started, you're welcome to check out Web Design Relief, a sister company of Writer's Relief.

PLUS—Are You Ready To Develop Your Author Platform?

Sign up on www.WebDesignRelief.com to get your free report, *The Writer's Essential Guide To Reputation-Building In A Digital World*, today! We are experts in designing websites specifically for authors. Check it out!

Having a website is an essential strategy; it's no longer optional for serious writers who want to make a name for themselves.

We know what works for author websites. And we're the *best* value on the Web for writers. We know—we did the research. Check out our website, and give us a call!

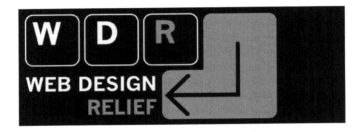

Our Invitation To You

Congratulations! You've finished reading *Publishing Poetry & Prose In Literary Journals*!

You now have the knowledge you need to build a successful personal submission strategy. We hope you'll refer to this book whenever you are in need of advice.

If we haven't answered a specific question, feel free to write to us using the contact form on our website. Thanks so much for reading our book. We truly hope we have been helpful to you.

Keep writing and submitting!

Ronnie L. Smith

Ronnie L. Smith and the Staff of Writer's Relief
www.WritersRelief.com
(866) 405-3003

Every writer suffers the writing blues at some point. And every *successful* writer finds a way through it. Intended for prose and poetry writers alike, *The Happy Writer* offers proven tips and motivational tools to overcome the practical and emotional issues you face as a writer.

Whether you're a new writer or a veteran author, finding a literary agent is the best hope for getting your book published. But, as any writer with a book project will tell you, capturing the attention and interest of a literary agent is easier said than done. You need a guide.

More information is available on our website store.

40915678R10071

Made in the USA
Lexington, KY
23 April 2015